The *Mary Celeste* and SS *Baychimo*: Th[e] Most Famous G[...]

By Charles River [Editors]

An 1861 painting of the *Mary Celeste*

About Charles River Editors

Charles River Editors is a boutique digital publishing company, specializing in bringing history back to life with educational and engaging books on a wide range of topics. Keep up to date with our new and free offerings with [this 5 second sign up on our weekly mailing list](), and visit [Our Kindle Author Page]() to see other recently published Kindle titles.

We make these books for you and always want to know our readers' opinions, so we encourage you to leave reviews and look forward to publishing new and exciting titles each week

Introduction

An engraving of the *Mary Celeste*

The *Mary Celeste*

"In the month of December in the year 1873, the British ship *Dei Gratia* steered into Gibraltar, having in tow the derelict brigantine Marie *Celeste*, which had been picked up in latitude 38 degrees 40', longitude 17 degrees 15' W. There were several circumstances in connection with the condition and appearance of this abandoned vessel which excited considerable comment at the time, and aroused a curiosity which has never been satisfied." – Sir Arthur Conan Doyle, "J. Habakuk Jephson's Statement"

People love mysteries, which is a good thing since history is so replete with them. This is especially true among seafaring people, and of all the mysteries of the deep, few rise to the level of the *Mary Celeste*.

In many ways, it is a story more suited for an episode of *The X-Files* than it is for any history book. There is the unlucky ship that began her sailing career under a cloud of bad fortune and accident. Then there is that handsome young captain, a man appearing to be of the highest moral fiber who chose to travel with his wife and young daughter rather than carouse with loose women. His crew was small but faithful, and his First Mate was an old friend. They set sail for Genoa late in 1872 but arrived instead in the history books, lost suddenly to a mystery that remains unsolved to this day.

The first indication that anything unusual had happened came on December 5 of that year, when the *Mary Celeste* was found by another ship, the *Dei Gratia*, sailing safely and intact but completely devoid of human beings. The bed was unmade and the captain's cabin a bit untidy, but otherwise there was no sign of struggle. Or was there? A sword turned up with spots that some thought must be blood, and there were also mysterious cuts on the ship's railing, but at the same time, the ship's provisions were almost entirely untouched, leading some to theorize pirates attacked the ship and others to believe all of it consisted of normal wear and tear?

The *Dei Gratia* towed the *Mary Celeste* and brought it to an admiralty court to seek a salvage prize, and eventually the court could find no evidence of foul play. At the same time, it awarded the crew of the *Dei Gratia* only a fraction of what the ship had been insured for, a suggestion that the court didn't completely believe the crew's account.

The mystery might have been forgotten altogether shortly after, but young Arthur Conan Doyle, who would eventually earn fame for his Sherlock Holmes mysteries, helped popularize the *Mary Celeste* and its mysterious fate with his fictional story "J. Habakuk Jephson's Statement." Naturally, as the story spread, so did the rumors and the theories. Some believed the crew mutinied, while others speculated that the boat's own owner had those on board killed. As the decades passed, men turned up claiming to have new information, but nothing definitive was ever confirmed. Given the mystery, over the years, whatever fear was trending in popular culture found its way into the *Mary Celeste* story. For example, sea monsters were blamed in the 19th century, and in the 20th century, some posited that aliens from outer space had captured the unfortunate passengers and swept them off to their home planet. While this might be among the less believable theories, none of the other theories can be completely proven either, ensuring that all of the theories (and new ones) will continue to form for as long as history remembers the story.

The SS *Baychimo*

By the early decades of the 20th century, the fur trade had tapered off some from its heyday in the 19th century, but it still proved profitable enough for hunters to live for months at a time in remote regions of Alaska. Their only contact with the outside world consisted of the company ships that came to buy their furs and bring them supplies.

One of these vessels was the steamer *Baychimo*, a Hudson's Bay Company ship that plied the treacherous waters off Alaska, Arctic Canada, and Siberia for many years, supplying remote outposts of Inuit and Anglo trappers and bringing back their catch of furs.

Her sailors were experts at handling Arctic waters, but one year the weather proved too much for them. In October of 1931, the *Baychimo* was carrying $1 million in furs for the Hudson's Bay Company when it was trapped by early winter pack ice in the Beaufort Sea. Ice is a powerful force of nature that can crush even the strongest of ships, so the captain had no choice but to order his crew of 14 men to unload all equipment essential for their survival and abandon the *Baychimo*. The cargo was too valuable to give up, however, so they retrieved lumber from the ship's carpentry stores with which to build a small house on the nearby ice. The captain hoped the ice would shift and free his vessel, at which point they could use one of the lifeboats to row back to the *Baychimo* and steam back home. In the worst-case scenario, they would have to spend the winter on the ice and wait for spring thaw. They wouldn't be the first Arctic crew to have done that. The Hudson's Bay Company airlifted out part of the crew, while the captain and remaining sailors hunkered down for a long wait, hoping the ice would break apart soon.

Nature had other ideas. On November 24, a month into their vigil, the crew had to hide inside their makeshift home as a fierce windstorm howled over the bleak icescape. However, when they could finally emerge into the daylight, they saw their ship had disappeared. An Inuit reported the *Baychimo* had drifted some 45 miles south and was once more trapped in the pack ice. The crew followed his directions to their wayward vessel, removing part of the cargo of furs. They presumed their ship would soon sink in the ice, so they trudged across the frozen wasteland back to civilization. It must have been an epic journey, but the *Baychimo* had started on an even greater one; the ship was still afloat, and began to travel with the currents. Inupiat hunters spotted it south of Barrow, and the following spring, a trapper found it trapped in the ice on the Beaufort Sea. He hadn't heard of the missing ship, and being curious, he boarded it. When he discovered it was a ghost ship, he left.

The ghost ship continued to be sighted in the region for years afterwards. In August of 1932, a group of Alaskan traders boarded her, exploring the abandoned galleys and cabins before leaving. The following March, a group of Inuit boarded her and got trapped for 10 days when a freak storm blew up. The last known boarding of the *Baychimo* occurred in November of 1939, when Captain Hugh Polson went aboard with the intention of salvaging her. He was soon driven off by encroaching pack ice.

The *Baychimo* continued to float in the waters between Alaska and Siberia, mostly in the Beaufort Sea. The latest confirmed report was by some Native Americans in 1969, between Barrow and Icy Cape, almost four decades after it had been lost. It's remarkable that it survived storms, pack ice, and encroaching rust after all that time. While it presumably sank sometime in 1969 or shortly thereafter, since it had been regularly reported up to that point and no reports exist after that final sighting, some believe the *Baychimo* still plies the Arctic waters somewhere, still carrying her cargo of furs.

The Mary Celeste and SS Baychimo: The Unsolved Mysteries of History's Most Famous Ghost Ships looks at some of the most famous maritime mysteries ever. Along with pictures of important people, places, and events, you will learn about the *Mary Celeste* and SS *Baychimo* like never before.

The *Mary Celeste* and SS *Baychimo*: The Unsolved Mysteries of History's Most Famous Ghost Ships

About Charles River Editors

Introduction

   Chapter 1: Amazon

   Chapter 2: An Interest in *Mary Celeste*

   Chapter 3: Something Was Wrong

   Chapter 4: Nothing to Account for the Disappearance of the Crew

   Chapter 5: The Sea Never Gives Up Its Secrets

The SS Baychimo

   Chapter 1: Successful Journeys

   Chapter 2: A Change of Luck

   Chapter 3: Final Voyages

   Chapter 4: 1931

   Chapter 5: The Ghost Ship

   Online Resources

   Bibliography

Free Books by Charles River Editors

Discounted Books by Charles River Editors

Chapter 1: Amazon

"The *Mary Celeste* was built at Spencer's Island in the Bay of Fundy, Nova Scotia. ... On the tenth of June, 1861, the vessel was registered at Parrsboro, in Nova Scotia, as a brigantine-rigged ship called the 'Amazon', with that name painted on her bows." – Stan Mason, *The Mary Celeste - Legend, Evidence and Truth*

The ship that will forever be known as the *Mary Celeste* was constructed in 1860 at Spencer's Island, Nova Scotia. Joshua Dewis, a local shipbuilder, owned the yard in which her keel was laid. She was a brigantine, with two masts and a hull built entirely out of hard Canadian lumber. When she was completed, she was launched on May 18, 1861, and christened the *Amazon*.

Dan Conlin's picture of Spencer's Island

Years later, George Spicer, who served as the ship's second mate for two years recalled that she "was launched down here on the beach just beside the mill, on a day in May. She was 184 tons burden, and was named the Amazon. Those men are making hay now on the spot where the builder got timber for the Amazon seventy-five years ago."

Nearly a month later, Dewis and eight other members of a local shipping company registered the ship in Parrsboro, giving its dimensions as just under 100 feet long, 25 and a half feet wide and nearly 12 feet deep, with nearly 200 gross tonnage. Historian Stan Mason offered more details: "She was built of beech, spruce, maple and birch woods, and the cabins were lined with pinewood. There were two masts: the foremost being square-rigged; the main mast 'fore and aft' (or schooner-rigged), which implies that the arrangement of sails were such that the leading edge of the fore and aft sails abutted the masts. The vessel was built with only one deck, a square stern, and carvel planking to produce a flush outward appearance. A carved scroll was sported under the bowsprit. The measurements were ninety-nine feet in length, twenty-five-and-a-half feet in breadth, and a depth of eleven-and-a-half feet. At that time, the gross tonnage was one hundred and ninety eight tons."

In early June 1861, Robert McLellan, himself a member of the company that owned the ship, took her out for her maiden voyage to Five Islands. The ship's first cargo was timber destined for London, but the trip had to be postponed because Captain McLellan fell ill while supervising the cargo being loaded. Instead, he returned to Spencer's Island, where he died on June 19. According to Spicer, "I sailed with the Amazon to Five Islands where she was to be loaded with deals for London...There was nothing unusual about the ship; she went along very well. I did not get any farther than Five Islands, that time, however, for I took sick and had to return home. The Amazon herself got no further than Quaco, near St John, New Brunswick. Captain McLellan took ill and they sailed back here. ... The Captain was brought up to our house where he passed away. He was sick only a few days. He was just a young man. We took his remains over to his home in Economy. I remember his young wife came down to the shore to see what was in the boat."

Captain John Parker took over for McLellan and completed the now apparently cursed voyage to London, but even before the ship had left North American waters, the *Amazon* hit a bundle of fishing equipment stored off the coast of Eastport, Maine. Robert Dewis, who served on the ship at that time, explained that misfortune and another one that struck in England: "We started on the voyage again (after McLellan's death) and for some reason I cannot recall we put into Eastport, Maine. On the way out of port we ran into some fish weirs in the Narrows and then lay for some days before we finally proceeded on our course across the Atlantic. We got to London, discharged the cargo and loaded another for Lisbon. On the way down the channel we ran into an English brig in the Strait of Dover and sunk her quickly, the crew climbing on board with us and all being saved. We put into Dover and landed our shipwrecks, repaired damages and resumed our voyage."

Perhaps to avoid further trouble in European waters, Parker kept the *Amazon* closer to home over the next few months, sailing her up and down the American coast to the West Indies. Then, in November 1861, the ship faced the Atlantic again, this time making for France. While there, the ship was featured in a painting by an unknown French artist, the only known contemporary depiction of the famous ship.

The *Amazon's* history remains largely unknown for the next year or two until 1863, when William Thompson took over as her captain. Spicer recalled, "I sailed as mate in the Amazon. We went to the West Indies, England and the Mediterranean – what we call the foreign trade. Not a thing unusual happened. We finally brought a load of corn from Baltimore to Halifax – Halifax imported corn then – and I came home to see the folks after a voyage of two years and three months in the Amazon. A week later, the Amazon had gone to Cow Bay, Cape Breton, to load coal for New York. There came a gale o' wind and she went ashore."

This last event happened in October at Cape Breton Island off the coast of North America. The ship was badly damaged and the consortium decided to abandon her to the rocks. A few days later, Alexander McBean purchased the wreck and requested legal ownership. This was granted in Halifax on October 14, 1867, with the court ruling, "It appears that the owners of the brigantine Amazon by power of attorney which, although not in accordance with the Registry Act, seems to be genuine and to have been regularly executed, authorized one William Thompson to sell and convey, said vessel then stranded at Glace Bay. It also appears that said vessel was sold and conveyed by said William Thompson to one Alexander McBean, the petitioner. This appears to have been a bona fide sale. I am therefore of the opinion that an order may be granted at once for the registry of said vessel at the Port of Halifax in the name of said Alexander McBean, the original name and number of said vessel being retained."

McBean quickly turned around and sold the ship, and while the next interim owner is unknown, he subsequently sold the ship to American Richard W. Haines of New York for $1,750.

After spending nearly $9,000 to restore the ship, Haines registered the ship in New York as the *Mary Celeste*, but unfortunately, Haines did not keep his prize for very long; in October 1869, his creditors seized it for payment of debts and sold it to a group of businessmen led by James Winchester. They kept the ship for another three years until 1872, when they spent $10,000 refitting and enlarging her. After that, several men of the consortium sold out their shares to Benjamin Spooner Briggs, the ship's new captain. For his part, Haines retained a controlling share of the ship.

Briggs was in his late 30s at the time he took command of the vessel, a married man who, with his wife, Sarah, had two children: seven year old Arthur and two year old Sophia. In Paul Begg's acclaimed book on the mystery, the historian described Briggs: "Benjamin grew up to be a responsible and respectable man who according to J. Franklin Briggs, in a letter to the great *Mary Celeste* historian Charles Edey Fay, 'spoke in a quiet tone of voice, and with an 'bore the highest character for seamanship and correctness' and in a letter to N.W. Bingham, Treasury Department Agent at Boston dated 3 April 1873, Sprague wrote that he had known Briggs for many years and that 'he always bore a good character as a Christian, and as an intelligent and active shipmaster.' By the 1870s Benjamin and his brother Oliver had tired of the sea and wanted to settle down to a normal life with their families ashore. The brothers considered combining their money in a small business. As related by Dr Oliver W. Cobb in his account of his family, Rose Cottage, Benjamin and Oliver wanted to take care of their growing families and planned to buy a hardware business in New Bedford, but at the last minute they recalled their father's disastrous business venture and reluctantly abandoned the idea. Oliver Briggs, who had bought some land and intended to buy a house, instead invested his money in a vessel named Julia A. Hallock, using his capital to undertake substantial repairs. Benjamin in 1872 invested his hardware store share in an interest in *Mary Celeste*."

Captain Briggs

Sarah Briggs

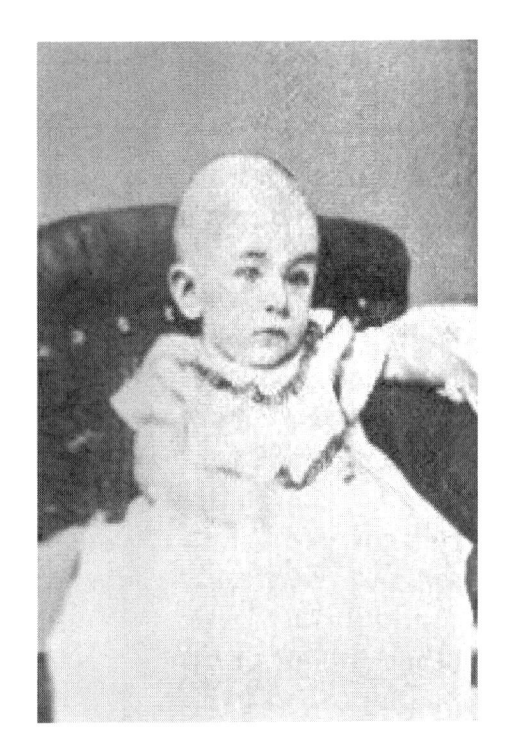

Sophia Briggs

Sarah and Arthur Briggs

A 19th century picture of New York Harbor

Chapter 2: An Interest in *Mary Celeste*

"I went down to the Marie *Celeste* that evening, and looked over my berth, which was extremely comfortable considering the small size of the vessel. Mr. Goring, whom I had seen in the morning, was to have the one next mine. Opposite was the captain's cabin and a small berth for Mr. John Harton, a gentleman who was going out in the interests of the firm. These little rooms were arranged on each side of the passage which led from the main-deck to the saloon. The latter was a comfortable room, the panelling tastefully done in oak and mahogany, with a rich Brussels carpet and luxurious settees." – Conan Doyle, *J.* "J. Habakuk Jephson's Statement"

In October 1872, Briggs travelled to New York to personally oversee the *Mary Celeste's* refitting. A week later, Sarah and Sophia joined him, while Arthur remained with his grandmother and attended school. One might wonder why Briggs brought his wife and his young daughter on board considering that he was carrying a dangerous cargo of 1,701 barrels of denatured alcohol which was known to be poisonous, but Briggs trusted himself, his vessel, and his crew, and he felt no cause for concern.

On November 3, Briggs wrote to his mother from New York, "It is a long time since I have written you a letter and I should like to give you a real interesting one but I hardly know what to say except that I am well and the rest of us ditto. … It seems to me to have been a great while since I left home but is only a little over two weeks but in that time my mind has been filled with business cares and I am again launched away into the busy whirl of business life from which I have so long been laid aside. For a few days it was tedious, perplexing, and very tiresome, but now I have got fairly settled down to it and it sits lightly and seems to run more smoothly and my appetite keeps good and I hope I shan't lose any flesh. It seems real home-like since Sarah and Sophia have got here and we enjoy our little quarters. On Thursday we have a call from Willie (Sarah's brother) and his wife. They took Sarah and Sophia with them on a ride up to Central Park. Sophia behaved splendidly and seemed to enjoy a ride as much as any of us. It is the only time they have been away from the vessel."

As if bad luck was stalking the *Mary Celeste* and the Briggs family, an epidemic of equine distemper was sweeping the city, keeping the young mother and child from being able to do any real sightseeing. Briggs explained, "On account of the Horse disease the horse-cars have not been running on this side of the city so we have not been able to go and make calls as we were so far away from anyone to go on foot, and to hire a private carriage would have cost us at least $ 10.00 a trip which we didn't feel able to pay and we couldn't walk and carry Sophia a mile or two which we should have had to to get to the ferry…"

In spite of this difficulty, Briggs painted a charming picture of family life as they all got set to board the doomed vessel: "It has been very confining for S. but I hope when we return we can make up for it. We seem to have a very good Mate and Steward and I hope shall have a pleasant voyage. We both have missed Arthur and I believe I should have sent for him if I could have thought of a good place to stow him away. Sophia calls for him occasionally and wants to see him in the Album which by the way is a favorite book of hers. She knows your picture in both Albums and points and says Gamma Bis. She seems real smart - has got over the bad cold she had when she came and has a first rate appetite for hash and bread and butter. I think the voyage will do her lots of good. We enjoy our melodeon and have some good sings, as I was in hope Oli (Benjamin's brother) might get in before I left but I'm afraid not now. We finished loading last night and shall leave on Tuesday morning if we don't get off tomorrow night, the Lord willing…Our vessel is in beautiful trim and I hope we shall have a fine passage, but as I have never been in her before I can't say how she'll sail."

Lastly, Briggs added some poignant personal notes, including a reference to their final destination of Genoa: "Shall want you to write us in about 20 days to Genoa, care of American Consul and about 20 days after to Messina care of American Consul who will forward to us if we don't get there. I wrote James (Benjamin's brother) to pay you for A's board and rent: if he forgets, call on him also for any money that may be necessary for clothes. Please get Eben to see his skates are all right and the holes in his new thick boot heels. I hope he'll keep well as I think if he does he'll be some help as well as company for you. Love to Hannah. Sophia calls Aunt Aunt Hannah often: I wish we had a picture so she could remember the countenance as well as name hoping to be with you again early in the spring."

Briggs had a small, handpicked crew with him when he left New York on November 7, 1872. He had sailed with his first mate, Albert Richardson, before, and his second mate was Andrew Gilling, then in his mid-20s. Newlywed Edward Head was his steward and came highly recommended by Winchester. Two brothers, Volkert and Boz Lorenzen, were part of the crew, while Gottlieb Goodschaad and Adrian Martens made up the rest.

Sarah wrote of the crew to her mother-in-law on November 7th, telling her, "Benj. thinks we have got a pretty peaceable set this time all around if they continue as they have begun. Can't tell yet how smart they are. B. reports a good breeze now, says we are going along nicely." Like her husband's letter, her final letter was full of affectionate familial tones: "Sophie thinks the figure 3 and the letter G. on her blocks is the same thing so I saw her whispering to herself yesterday with the 3 block in her hand - Gam-Gam-Gamma. … I should like to be present at Mr. Kingsbury's ordination next week. Hope the people will be united with him, and wish we might hear of Mrs. K's improved health on arrival. Tell Arthur I make great dependence on the letter I shall get from him, and will try to remember anything that happens on the voyage which he would be pleased to hear. We had some baked apples (sour) the other night about the size of a new-born infant's head. They tasted extremely well. Please give our love to Mother and the girls, Aunt Hannah, Arthur and other friends, reserving a share for yourself."

Sarah also gave left the only extant record of the *Mary Celeste's* departure: "[I]nstead of proceeding to sea when we came out Tuesday morning, we anchored about a mile or so from the city, as it was a strong headwind, and B. said it looked so thick and nasty ahead we shouldn't gain much if we were beating and banging about. Accordingly we took a fresh departure this morning with wind light but favorable, so we hope to get outside without being obliged to anchor. Have kept a sharp look-out for Oliver but so far have seen nothing of him. It was rather trying to lay in sight of the city for so long and think that most likely we had letters waiting for us there, and be unable to get them. However, we hope no great change has occurred since we did hear and shall look for a goodly supply when we reach G[enoa]."

Richardson

Chapter 3: Something Was Wrong

"[T]he Marie Celeste may have been abandoned a considerable distance from the spot at which she was picked up, since a powerful current runs up in that latitude from the African coast. He confesses his inability, however, to advance any hypothesis which can reconcile all the facts of the case." – Conan Doyle, J. "J. Habakuk Jephson's Statement"

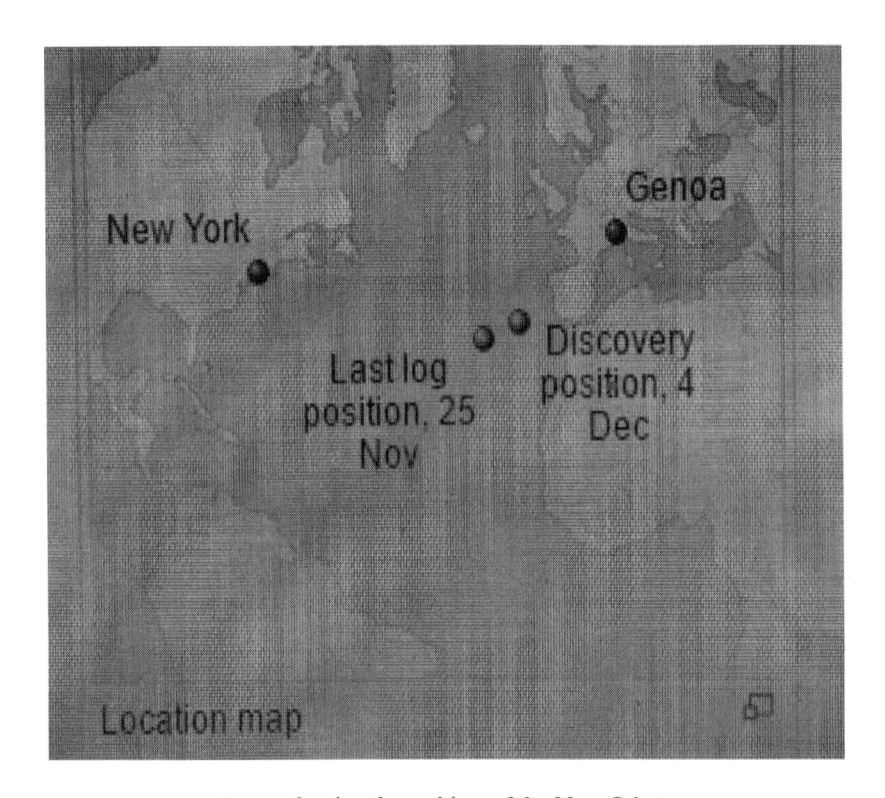

A map showing the positions of the *Mary Celeste*

When the *Mary Celeste* departed, it was the last time anyone on board was ever seen or heard from again. Instead, at about mid-day in early December 1872, a few weeks after the ship had departed, she was found floating in open water about halfway between Portugal and the Azores. In *Mary Celeste: The Greatest Mystery of the Sea*, Paul Begg described the scene when the *Mary Celeste* was discovered by another ship, the *Dei Gratia*: "It was on Wednesday, 4 December 1872 land time or Thursday, 5 December 1872 sea time that *Dei Gratia* sighted *Mary Celeste*. It isn't clear who first sighted the derelict. According to John Wright, second mate of *Dei Gratia*, seaman John Johnson was at the wheel and sighted *Mary Celeste* off the port bow at about 1.00 p.m. sea time and the state of the vessel's sails had caught his curiosity. Johnson had then called to Wright and pointed out the vessel. However, Captain Morehouse also claimed to have been the first to sight the vessel. He had just come on deck and had noticed the *Celeste*, which he judged to have been about six miles distant. Morehouse and Johnson probably saw her simultaneously. *Mary Celeste* was bearing east-north-east, steering west-south-west on a starboard tack, whilst *Dei Gratia* was steering south-east-half-east on a port tack – in other words, *Mary Celeste* was sailing towards *Dei Gratia*. Captain Morehouse studied the distant stranger through his glass and saw as Johnson had done that she carried little sail. Morehouse concluded that something was wrong and ordered *Dei Gratia* to sail toward her. Fifteen or twenty minutes later it was clear that *Mary Celeste* was yawing and Morehouse also thought he could see a flag of distress at her yard (it was in fact a flapping sail). He called Oliver Deveau, the mate, who was off duty below deck, who viewed the ship and immediately agreed with Morehouse that the vessel was in trouble."

Captain Morehouse of the *Dei Gratia* recorded the discovery in his log: "December 5. Begins with a fresh breeze and clear, sea still running heavy but wind moderating. Saw a sail to the E. 2 p.m. Saw she was under very short canvas, steering very wild and evidently in distress. Hauled up to speak her and render assistance, if necessary. At 3 p.m. hailed her and getting no answer and seeing no one on deck ... out boat and sent the mate and two men on board, sea running high at the time. He boarded her without accident and returned in about an hour and reported her to be the *Mary Celeste*, at and from New York, for Genoa, abandoned with 3 ½ ft. of water in hold."

Second Mate John Wright elaborated on the spotting of the ship: "It was…during my watch that we sighted the derelict. The man at the wheel named Johnson first sighted her and he called to me and showed me the vessel. Our head was then S.E. by E. the head of the other vessel was N.W. by N. as far as I could judge. She was on our port bow. When I first saw the vessel it was the state of the vessel's sails that caught my attention. I am sure she had her lower top foresail set. She had no after sail on. I should say it was about 2 hours from time of first seeing her to lowering boat to board her. She yawed some but not much, that also attracted my attention. I did not particularly notice the state of her masts and yards they were all standing the Royal was bent and furled. I saw the rigging was out of order, the standing rigging wanted getting up and rattling down, the running rigging I did not notice. I did not notice the state of the peak Halyards."

Oliver Deveau was sent by Morehouse with Wright to explore the ship and later testified, "By my reckoning we were 38 ° 20 N. Lat 17 ° 15 West Longitude by dead reckoning of our own ship. … The sea was running high, the weather having been stormy, though then the wind was moderating. I boarded the vessel and the first thing I did was to sound the pumps, which were in good order. I found no one on board the vessel. I found the forehatch and the lazaret hatch both off, the binnacle stove in a great deal of water between the decks, the forward house full of water up to the combing (the forward house is on the upper deck). I found everything wet in the cabin in which there had been a great deal of water, the clock was spoilt by the water, the sky light of the cabin was open and raised, the compass in the binnacle was destroyed. I found all the Captains effects had been left. I mean his clothing furniture &c the bed was just as they had left it. The bed and other clothes were wet. I judged that there had been a woman on board. I found the Captain's Charts and Books a number of them, in the Cabin; some were in two bags under the bed and some (two or three) loose charts over the bed. I found no charts on the table. I found the log book and the log slate. I found the log book in the mate's cabin on his desk, the log slate I found on the Cabin table."

According to Wright, the men were badly hampered in their investigation by the lack of light.

He explained, "I should say about 10 inches above the deck the only way of lighting the cabin is by the skylight and the windows three on each side of the cabin and by the companion when the door is open, the windows were nailed up on the starboard side with plank, they were not nailed up on port side, the windows were shut on port side and would let the light in I could not say whether the windows were fastened up for the voyage, or had been fastened during the voyage. On the starboard side the planking was nailed outside the glass on the port side the windows were shut with glass only and were not broken. When below in the cabin there was plenty of light to see what was on the table."

While investigating the ship, Deveau found what he believed was the first clue as to what had happened. "I found an entry in the log book up to the 24th November and an entry on the log slate dated 25th November showing that they had made the Island of Saint Mary. I did not observe the entry on the slate the first day and made some entries of my own on it and unintentionally rubbed out the entry when I came to use the slate at least I thought so. I did not find the ship' Register or other papers concerning the ship but only some letters and account books. I found the mate's book in which were entered receipts for Cargo &c. The book now shown me is the book I found, also the Mate's Chart in his cabin hanging over the mate's bed showing the track of the vessel up to the 24th. There were two charts in the mate's cabin, one under the mate's bed and as I have said hanging over it. I am not positive whether the chart with the ship's track marked on it was found above or below the mate's bed. ... The *Mary Celeste* has only two hatches fore and main besides the lazarets. The Cabin of the *Mary Celeste* is lightly raised above the upper deck about 2 feet above and the windows are in those two feet, there were five windows, 2 in the Captains, 1 in Mate, 1 in W.C. and one in pantry they were all battened up with canvas and boards."

Knowing now that Briggs and his crew had been gone from the ship less than 10 days, Deveau looked around for more clues. He explained, "There seemed to be everything left behind in the cabin as if left in a great hurry but everything in its place. I noticed the impression in the Captain's bed as of a child having lain there. The hull of the vessel appeared in good condition and nearly new. There were a great many other things in the cabin but impossible for me to mention all, the things were all wet, the sky light was not off but open, the hatches were off, the cabin was wet but had no water in it the water had naturally run out of it, the hull of the ship was apparently new, the masts were good, the spars all right, the rigging in very bad order, some of the running rigging carried away gone, the standing rigging was all right, the upper foretopsail and foresail gone apparently blown away from the yards. Lower foretopsail hanging by the four corners. Main stay sail hauled down and laying on the forward house loose as if it had been let run down, jib and foretop stay sail set, all the rest of the sails being furled. The vessel is a Brigantine rigged I should say was sea worthy and almost a new vessel. Anchors and chains all right, there were not boats and no davits at the side. I don't think she used davits. It appeared as if she carried her boat on deck, there was a spar lashed across the stern davits so that no boat had been there."

Part of his search of the ship led Deveau to the ship's galley, where he discovered everything in order. He claimed, "On the table there was the log slate but I cannot state what else there might be on the table. I do not know whether there were any knives. I saw no preparation made for eating in the Cabin, there was plenty to eat, but all the knives and forks were in the pantry. The rack was on the table but no eatables. There was nothing to eat or drink in the cabin on the table, but preserved meats in the pantry. I examined the state of the ship's galley. It was in the corner of the forward house and all the things, pots, kettle, &c were washed up, water in the house a foot or so deep. I cannot say how the water got in but the door was open and the scuttle hatch off, the windows were shut. There were no cooked provisions in the galley. … There was a barrel of flour in the galley one third gone. We used the provisions found on board the *Mary Celeste*. We used potatoes and meat, she had I should say six months provisions on board, I fixed it and used it on our way here. The glass was broken, the binnacle was washed away from its place and I set it back again. It is lashed on the top of the cabin above the deck being a wooden one, the lashing had given away one of the cleats was gone. I found a compass on board afterwards, the Cabin compass in the mate's room. I did not find until I went on board a second time. It is usual for the vessel to carry two or three compasses. I found quadrants, one in the second Mate's room. I made no further examination of the cargo than what I have already stated, the cargo seemed to be in good condition and well stowed and had not shifted, as far as I could judge the cargo was not injured. I found no wine beer or spirits whatever in the ship." This last piece of observation was in keeping with Briggs' character: he was a devout teetotaler.

During his inspection, Deveau also found evidence of the captain's family life, explaining, "I have said that there was the appearance on the bed in the Captain's Cabin as if a child had slept in it, there was room in berth for a child and a woman and also for the Captain. I saw articles of Child's wearing apparel also Child's toys. The bed was as it had been left being slept in not made. I noticed female clothing, an old dress hanging near the bed, also India rubber over shoes. The dress was dirty as if worn not wet, the bedding was wet. I should say that the water had got through the windows near the bed or probably it might have got through the sky light, the windows were battened up. There had been rain and squalls the morning we found the *Mary Celeste* but I don't think it was that which had wetted the bed. There were two boxes of clothing. In one box male and female clothing mixed together. The box was shut but not locked, the clothing was not wet. The other box had only remnants of cloth in it. Both boxes were open. I afterwards found some clothing in the drawers, which I also afterwards took out and put into the second box which was nearly empty. The clothing found under the bed place were mostly men's clothing and some of it was wet. That found in the lower drawer, the clothing was of the usual sort worn by men and women."

It was obvious that a woman had been on board by the items she left behind. Deveau continued, "There was also work bags with needles, threads, buttons, books and case of instruments, a dressing case and other things in the drawers. The two boxes were in the cabin, there was also a valise which I could open, there was also a writing desk there was a bag of dirty clothing, man's, woman's and child's hanging up in the water closet. They were damp, I cannot say how they got damp. There was a stove in the forecabin but I made no fire in it, there were a few old coats and a pair of boots, also the clothes were not those of a passenger but of a seafaring man. The stove was in the forecabin not in the Captains Cabin. There was a swinging lamp on the side of the cabin, one in each cabin, they were paraffin lamps. There was no appearance of damage by fire nor any appearance of fire or smoke in any part of the ship. The stay sail which had fallen down was of the stove pipe of the galley. There was plenty of provisions and plenty of water on board the vessel. There was a harmonium or melodium in the cabin."

Deveau also looked into the sailors' quarters, where he found what seemed to be further clues: "There were four berths in the forecastle with bedding in the *Celeste* but only three sea chests. Often two sailors chum for one chest, the bedding was damp as if it had been used. There was one berth in the Mate's cabin and one berth in the galley also a berth in the second mate's room or boatswain's room all apparently had been occupied with the Captain making eight all told besides the woman and child. She was sheeted on the starboard tack when we found her. The wind during the last four days before we found the vessel was North Westerly the men's clothing was all left behind their oilskins boots and even their pipes as if they had left in a great hurry or haste. My reason for saying they to0 have left in haste is that a sailor would generally take such things especially his pipe if not in great haste. The Chronometer the Sextant and Navigation book were all absent the ship's Register and papers also not found. There was no log line ready for use, the Carpenters tools were in the mate's room the water casks were on chocks the chocks had been moved as if struck by a heavy sea the provision casks were below in their proper place they were not thrown over. If the vessel had been capsized they would have been thrown over."

Devau continued to look around the ship, and with each passing discovery, it seemed more and more that everyone must have left the ship suddenly and gone off in the life boat. He cited one potential factor for the abandonment: "The only explanation of the abandonment which I can give is that there was a panic from the belief that the vessel had more water in her than she had as afterwards proved."

As Begg explained in his history of the ship, this is a reference to the fact that there was about three and a half feet of standing water in the hold, but it had obviously stayed afloat for seemingly 10 days after being abandoned, and the men of the *Dei Gratia* would subsequently demonstrate that the *Mary Celeste* didn't seem to actually be taking on water: "Oliver Deveau knew from the experience of sailing *Mary Celeste* into Gibraltar that she took on very little water. He therefore concluded that the 3 ½ feet found in the hold had to have entered over the decks and through the open hatches and cabin. We can further surmise that the sounding rod discarded on the deck indicates that the vessel had been sounded at the time of or immediately after whatever had caused the abandonment, and if the latter then it is reasonable to suppose that whatever had happened had given rise to concern that the ship was taking on water. The water, then, was a contributory factor in the abandonment of *Mary Celeste* – the captain and crew thought she was sinking! ... In the Captain's cabin Deveau found Captain Briggs's charts and books, some in two bags under the bed, and two or three loose charts over the bed. There were no charts on the table. The bed was unmade, as if just vacated by its occupants, and bore the impression on the mattress of a child having been asleep in it – these unmade beds being further indications that disaster had struck *Mary Celeste* in early morning. The bedding was wet, Deveau thought probably by water that had come through the open skylight or somehow through the boarded-up windows near the bed."

Deveau also noted there was initially a debate over whether the *Mary Celeste* had a lifeboat, and whether it had been launched: "There were no spare spars on the decks of the *Mary Celeste* whatever. When there is no boat on the davits in the stern there is often a spar lashed to keep the davits steady. In this case the spar was lashed thro' the sheave holes which showed there had been no boat there. We had two boats, the *Celeste* had not accommodation on deck for two boats. One could see where the boat had been lashed across the main hatch but that was not the right place for her there were no lashings visible therefore I cannot swear that the *Mary Celeste* had any boat at all but there were two fenders where the boat would be lashed. Assuming that there was a boat there was nothing to show how the boat was launched there were no signs of any tackles to launch her."

Even as the crew of *Dei Gratia* pondered what caused the ship to be abandoned, they also knew there was no way anyone was going to answer that question in the middle of the ocean. Deveau recalled what he reported back to his own captain: "I went back to my own vessel and reported the state of the Brigantine to the Captain. I proposed taking her in, he told me well to consider the matter as there was great risk and danger to our lives and also to our own vessel. We consulted amongst ourselves and crew and resolved to bring her in a distance I estimate at six to seven hundred miles, but have not made out the exact distance. The Captain gave me two men, a small boat, a barometer compass and watch. I took with me my own nautical instruments and whatever food our steward had prepared and I went on board the same afternoon, the 5th, about an hour afterwards perhaps, hoisted the boat on deck, pumped her out and took charge of the vessel. .... We arrived in Gibraltar on the morning of the 13th December. When we first went on board we had a good deal to do to get the ship into order. I found a spare trysail which I used as a foresail. It took me two days to set things to rights so as to proceed on the voyage to make any headway. ... When I arrived at Gibraltar I found the *Dei Gratia* already here. I had seen her almost every day during the voyage and spoke her three or four times. We kept company with her until the night of the storm when I lost sight of her. I saw between decks the nature of the cargo-barrels marked alcohol on the head of them and likewise in the note book of a mate of the *Celeste* whereby it appeared he had given receipts for so many barrels of alcohol at a time. I forgot to state that the cabin which was a deck cabin had all its windows battened up. I also found the sounding rod on deck alongside the pump."

A 19th century depiction of Gibraltar

Chapter 4: Nothing to Account for the Disappearance of the Crew

"'We have ourselves,' says the anonymous writer in the Gazette, 'been over the derelict *Marie Celeste*, and have closely questioned the officers of the *Dei Gratia* on every point which might throw light on the affair. They are of opinion that she had been abandoned several days, or perhaps weeks, before being picked up…There is no reference to rough weather, and, indeed, the state of the vessel's paint and rigging excludes the idea that she was abandoned for any such reason. She is perfectly watertight. No signs of a struggle or of violence are to be detected, and there is absolutely nothing to account for the disappearance of the crew.'" – Conan Doyle, *J.* "J. Habakuk Jephson's Statement"

As soon as the *Dei Gratia* arrived in Gibraltar, Captain Morehouse sent news of his discovery to the Atlantic Mutual Insurance Company, which duly recorded, "Found fourth and brought here '*Mary Celeste*' abandoned seaworthy admiralty impost notify all parties telegraph offer of salvage. Morehouse."

Meanwhile, Horatio Sprague, United States Consul, telegraphed the Board of Underwriters in New York, "Brig '*Mary Celeste*' here derelict important send power attorney to claim her from admiralty court." He also informed the American Consul of what had happened. Meanwhile, the British newspaper, Lloyd's List reported, "Gibraltar, Dec. 13, 1872, 1.45 P.M. – The *Mary Celeste* (Aust. brigantine), from New York to Genoa, with alcohol, has been derelict at sea and brought here by three men of the *Dei Gratia* (British brigantine). Gibraltar, Dec. 14, 1872. – The

Mary Celeste (British brigantine) is in possession of the Admiralty Court."

The Admiralty court wasted no time in meeting, and Sir James Cochrane, then the Chief Justice of Gibraltar, called the proceedings to order on December 17, 1872. He was well-respected in his field, with one of his contemporaries writing of him, "During the long time that Sir James Cochrane has presided over the supreme court at Gibraltar he has eminently maintained the high character of the bench. The clearness of his judgment, the wisdom of his decisions, and his personal character have commanded the respect of all classes of the community. He has done much for the lower classes, and his firmness and perfect fairness have helped greatly to dispel from the city of Gibraltar the crime of using the knife, which was unfortunately once so prevalent." Attorney General of Gibraltar Frederick Solly Flood acted as the chief investigator on behalf of the Crown.

Cochrane's house

Flood

The court ordered an inspection made of the ship itself, with a diver inspecting the hull of the ship below the water line. John Austin, who executed the inspection for the court, prepared a lengthy report that insisted the ship could not have come in contact with bad weather. "On the Starboard side of the main cabin was the chief mate's cabin, on a little bracket in which I found a small phial of oil for a sewing machine in its proper perpendicular position a reel of cotton for such a machine and a thimble. If they had been there in bad weather then they wd. have been thrown down or carried away."

Based on what he saw, Austin concluded, "The Vessel was thoroughly sound staunch and strong & not making water to any appreciable extent. I gave directions to Ricardo Portunato an experienced Diver minutely & carefully to examine the whole of the hull and bottom of the said Vessel her stem, keel, Sternpost & rudder while I was engaged on board in surveying her, and he remained under water for that purpose for a time amply sufficient for that purpose. I have now perused and considered the paper writing marked A produced & shown to me at the time of the swearing this my affidavit & which purports to be an affidavit by said Ricardo Portunato in this cause on the 7th day of Jany. now instant. Having carefully weighed & considered the contents thereof & all & singular the matters aforesaid I am wholly unable to discover any reason whatever why the said Vessel should have been abandoned."

Austin did find one item, mentioned to him previously by some of the men who had inspected the ship initially, that pointed to foul play. He noted, "I also observed in this cabin a Sword in its scabbard which the Marshall informed me he had noticed when he came on board for the purpose of arresting the vessel. It had not [word missing] affected by water but on drawing out the blade it appeared to me as if it had been smeared with blood and afterwards wiped."

Dr. J. Patron, who examined the supposed blood, presented an analysis for the court in January 1873: "At the request of Her Majesty's Attorney General I proceeded on board of the American brig *Mary Celeste* anchored in this Bay for the purpose of ascertaining whether any marks or stains of blood could be discovered on or in her hulk. After a careful and minute inspection of the deck of the said vessel some red brown spots about a millimetre thick and half an inch in diameter with a dull aspect were found on deck in the forepart of the vessel these spots were separated with a chissel [sic] and carefully wrapped in paper No. 1. Some other similar spots were equally gathered in different parts of the deck and wrapped in papers numbered, 2, 3, and 4. Paper No. 5 contained a powder grated from a suspicious mark seen on the topgallant rail part of which was obtained on board and part from a piece of timber belonging to the said vessel in Her Majesty's Attorney General chambers. I carefully examined the cabin both with natural and artificial light; the floor, the sides of the berths, mattrasses [sic] etc. were minutely searched and nothing worth calling attention was seen that could have any relation with the object of my enquiries. On the 31st January at 2 o'clock I received from the hands of Mr. Vecchio Marshal of the Supreme Court the five papers above mentioned and numbered 1, 2, 3, 4, and 5 and a sword with its sheath found on board the said vessel."

After hearing testimony from Deveau, Wright, and others, the court remained inconclusive about what happened to the *Mary Celeste*, thus leaving the door wide open for speculation. For his part, Flood believed there was some sort of foul play, even after an expert on the subject tested the "blood spots" and declared, "I feel myself authorized to conclude that according to our present scientific knowledge there is no blood either in the stains observed on the deck of the *Mary Celeste* or on those found on the blade of the sword that I have examined."

Within a few days, rumors had spread across the Atlantic, and speculation was rife about what had happened to the ship. The *Shipping and Commercial List* reported on December 21, "The strange feature about the *Mary Celeste* is the fact that she was in seaworthy condition. There was no evidence that she had been run into, or that she had encountered unusually heavy weather. The inference is that there has been foul play somewhere, and that alcohol is at the bottom of it." But a few days later, on December 25, the paper clarified its report, explaining, "In our last issue we noted the fact, based on private despatches, that the brig *Mary Celeste*, hence for Genoa with a cargo of Alcohol, had been abandoned, and subsequently fallen in with and towed into Gibraltar; that as the vessel when found was in a seaworthy condition, apprehensions of foul play were entertained, and that Alcohol was probably at the bottom of it. It seems that the closing sentence of the paragraph was misconstrued into a reflection upon the honesty or good faith of the shippers, although it really bore no such interpretation. The shippers of the cargo of the *Mary Celeste* are known to us as being among the most honorable of firms, and not the slightest suspicion is entertained of fraud on their part, so far as we are aware. The impression we intended to convey was that the crew had possibly been making free with the Alcohol, and that foul play had resulted. This, of course, is mere conjecture, and until the affair has been fully investigated, the real cause of abandonment cannot be known – perhaps it never will be."

On January 22, 1873, Flood sent a damning report to the Board of Trade in which he asserted, "My own theory or guess is that the crew got at the alcohol and in the fury of drunkenness murdered the Master whose name was Briggs and wife and child and the Chief Mate, that they then damaged the bows of the vessel with the view of giving it the appearance of having struck on rocks or suffered from a collision so as to induce the Master of any vessel which might pick them up if they saw her at some distance to think her not worth attempting to save, and that they did sometime between the 25th Novbr. and the 5th Decbr. escape on board some vessel bound for some North or South American port or the West Indies." There were a number of problems with this theory, of course, not the least of which was that there was no sign of any liquor found on the ship, in keeping with Briggs' policy of abstinence.

By the time Flood filed his report, James Winchester had reached Gibraltar with the intension of claiming his cargo. Flood wanted Winchester to post $15,000 as a bond, and when Winchester complained, it came to light that Flood suspected him of having Briggs, his family and his men killed. Before long, however, so much evidence had come to light to discredit Flood that his accusations were largely dismissed, so Flood released the *Mary Celeste* to Winchester on February 25, 1873. Early the following month, the ship sailed away for Genoa with a new captain, George Blatchford, at her wheel.

On April 8, Cochrane awarded Morehouse and his crew £1,700, for the salvage, only about 20% of the total value of the ship and its cargo. Begg wrote of these results, "On 14 March 1873, four days after *Mary Celeste* sailed from Gibraltar, Chief Justice Cochrane delivered judgment in the salvage case. *Mary Celeste* was valued at $ 5,700.00 and her cargo at $ 36,943.00, making a total of $ 42,673.00. The salvers were awarded £ 1,700, less the costs of the analysis of the bloodstains which was deducted from that amount. It was considerably less than what they no doubt expected and rightfully should have received, and the crew of *Dei Gratia* and her owners were apparently and understandably very angry and disappointed. It was no doubt with a heavy heart that Oliver Deveau took command of *Dei Gratia* on 17 March and sailed from Genoa to Messina. She arrived there on 21 March and on her arrival a painting of the ship was made. The ship sailed soon after, and after a brief stop at Gibraltar she sailed for New York, reaching her home port on 19 June. On 19 November Consul Sprague notified the Department of State that he had dispatched the effects of Captain and Mrs Briggs to the United States and on 11 December the Collector of Customs in New York made a report that they had been received safe and sound. We don't know what happened to them all, including the crew's five chests and a canvas bag, but we know that Mrs Briggs's sewing machine and beloved melodeon reached the home of Benjamin's mother, as did the Italian sword, the stain on which had caused so much trouble. "

Even with the case adjudicated, rumors about what actually happened to the ship's crew continued to spread. *The Times of London* told readers on February 14, "As regards the interior of the ship – a very minute survey showed most clearly that not only had the vessel not sustained any accident, but that she could not have encountered any seriously heavy weather. The whole of the hull, masts and yards were in good condition, and the pitch in the water-ways had not started, which must have been the case had any bad weather been experienced. The deck-house, made of thin planking and 6ft in height above the deck, was perfect, there not being a crack in the planking nor even in the paint. The seaman's chests and clothing found on board were perfectly dry, some razors even being quite free from rust. ... Spare panes of glass were also found stowed away and unbroken. All the articles of furniture in the captain's cabin, including a harmonium, were in their proper places and uninjured by water, the music and other books also being dry."

After reviewing the facts, the article drew its own conclusion: "No bills of lading nor manifest was found on board. The effects found in the captain's cabin were of considerable value and proved that a lady and child had been on board. The ship's log, which was found on board, showed that the last days work of the ship was on 24th of November, sea time, when the weather allowed an observation to be taken which placed the vessel at lat. 36.56 N., long. 27.20 W. The entries on the log slate were, however, carried on up to 8 a.m. on the 25th, at which time the vessel passed from west to east to the north of the island of Saint Mary's (Azores), the eastern point of which at 8 a.m. bore S.S.L six miles distant. The distance of the longitude of the places where the *Mary Celeste* was found from that of the island of Saint Mary's is 7.54. E., and the corrected distance of the latitude from the position last indicated in the log is 1.18 N., so that the vessel had apparently held on her due course for 10 days after the 25th of November, the wheel being loose all the time. But the log of the *Dei Gratia* shows that during this time, from the 25th of November to the day when she met with the *Mary Celeste*, the 5th of December, the wind was more or less from the north, and that she was on a port tack during the whole of that period. It appears, therefore, almost impossible that the derelict should have compassed the same time and distance of 7.54 L, at all events on the starboard tack, upon which she was met by the *Dei Gratia*, and the obvious inference is that she was not abandoned until some days after the last entry made in the log. Naturally, various theories are set up to account for this extraordinary series of facts, and the finding of the sword and the blood stains are held to point to some deed of violence."

Some immediately believed that pirates must surely be to blame, as noted by the *New York Times* in a report on February 27, 1873: "And yet it is now announced that a New England vessel, the brig *Mary Celeste*, of Marion, Mass., was seized by pirates in the Atlantic during the Fall of 1872. The brig was fallen in with by a British vessel last November in good condition, and yet entirely deserted. She had sailed…weeks previously from Boston for Genoa…. That she was deserted is alone but scant evidence that her commander had been foully dealt with, for, had he voluntarily abandoned her in order to defraud the underwriters, he would certainly have taken the precaution to sink or destroy her. Other evidence, however, was not wanting that a great crime had been committed. The cabin was in a disordered condition, and had evidently been ransacked…. The conclusion seems inevitable that the crew had mutinied; that after they had seized the brig, murdered the Captain, his wife, and probably the subordinate officers, and taken to the boats. … Nevertheless, there can hardly be a doubt that the boats which were missing when the abandoned *Mary Celeste* was found, had left her side bearing a company of … cutthroats for whom every civilized nation has a gallows in waiting. It is thought that the pirates would have shaped their course toward the Azores. No report of their binding has, however, been received, and it is quite possible that they have fallen victims to the vengeance of the elements, or that, ignorant of navigation, they have lost their way, and perished miserably of exposure and starvation. … Probably they will never be found, but the fate of the *Mary Celeste* remains to remind us that piracy is not yet obsolete even on the Atlantic, and that the doom of those who, in by-gone years, were made to walk the plank may have been repeated in the person of a Yankee and his delicate wife."

In the early stages of the ongoing mystery, there was still hope that the *Mary Celeste*'s passengers would end up being accounted for or heard from, as evidenced by a report in the *Boston Daily Globe* on February 29: "It was stated some time since that the brig Mary Cleste, Capt. Benj. Briggs, which left New York Nov 17 for Genoa, with a cargo of alcohol, had been picked up abandoned…. The supposition being that she had been in collision and that her crew had been taken off by some vessel unknown, but no tidings have yet been received from them, and some apprehension exists as to their safety. They may, however, have gone onboard a vessel bound on a distant voyage, in which case sufficient time has not yet elapsed to hear of their arrival. … Capt Briggs, who belongs in Marion. Mass., had his wife and child on board and as many things were found in confusion on the vessel, including ladies' apparel, this circumstance has added to the suspicion of some outrage on the part of the crew. They were mostly foreigners, and in ease of mutiny by breaking into her cargo, the men might have become inflamed by the liquor to the commission of murder. It is hoped that the first supposition may prove correct, and that the officers and crew will yet be heard from. The brig remains in the hands of the Admiralty Court at Gibraltar."

The Globe updated its readers on the case a few days later, writing on March 4, "The cargo, consisting of barrels of spirits, is untouched, with the exception of one cask which had started. The rear ensigns of the vessel having suffered from bad weather in any respect, the most minute examination having failed to detect any injury above water or below it. ... There are marks like sharp cuts on the top gallant rail, and on both sides of the vessel's bows, which appear to have been done on purpose; whether tills points to any act of violence, and with what motive committed—why the vessel was left under sail in the apparent absence either of plunder or of peril, why she was ever deserted at all—is still an absolute mystery..."

On March 10, the *Madison Wisconsin State Journal* admitted that one much grislier scenario could explain the mystery: "Conjectures in regard to the true cause of her abandonment are, of course, likely to be pretty fertile, but the probable hypothesis is that for some reason the crew revolted, murdered the captain and his passengers, and then took to flight, carrying away with them nothing which might lead to their arrest and conviction."

As time passed, it became clear that the claims of the bloody sword were in fact nothing more than rumors and speculation. On April 4, the American wire services reported, "The New York Tribune says that Mr. Winchester, the owner of the brigantine *Mary Celeste*, found abandoned at sea in December last, says that upon learning of the abandonment the vessel he went to Gibraltar and examined the vessel thoroughly, and stated that there were no signs of blood either on the sails or the sword, as mentioned in the circular. The stains on the sails were from service, and those on the sword from rust. The alleged impairment of the bows arose from the action of the atmosphere and the water on the hard pine planking. Mr. Winchester attributes the disappearance of Captain Briggs, his wife, child and crew to the grounding of the vessel, when, fearing to be lost, he abandoned her."

Ultimately, the mystery remained, leaving the April 14 edition of the *Salt Lake Daily Tribune* to turn to a famous superstitious tale about the high seas: "What can be the matter with the crews of American vessels that they thus abandon their ships and vanish into the unknown? Their vessels were not abandoned because they could no longer protect their crews from the elements. Neither could the motive of their abandonment have been a desire to defraud the insurance companies, for in that case the vessels would have been scuttled. Can it be that the Flying Dutchman has crossed the Equator in search of forced recruits for his venerable crew?"

Even as these and other stories were being published and read, the *Mary Celeste* was back on the open seas. After unloading her cargo in Genoa, the ship finally returned home, arriving in New York on September 19, 1873. There she sat for some time, as no one wanted to take a chance on such a seemingly unlucky vessel. Finally, in February 1874, the owners sold her at a discount to an American businessman who was more interested in a bargain than he was in superstition.

Over the next several years, the *Mary Celeste* sailed primarily in the area in and around the Indian Ocean, where bad luck continued to follow her. Her captain, Edgar Tuthill, became ill in February 1879 and died before he could return home. The following year, a businessman named Wesley Gove bought the ship, along with a number of other Bostonians, and put a new captain,

Thomas Fleming, in place. He seemed to have better luck than the previous men and survived long enough to pass the ship off to Gilman Parker in 1884.

While some captains wanted to avoid thinking about the potential of a curse upon the ship, Parker tried to use it to his advantage when he sailed for Port-au-Prince, Haiti, on December 16 with a load of overinsured cargo. He then ran the ship aground just off the coast, and after he and his crew were able to easily abandon the ship and make their way to the mainland, he filed his insurance claim. Fortunately, he was caught and forced to repay what he had been given, but with the deed having been done, the *Mary Celeste* lay in pieces on the Rochelois reef.

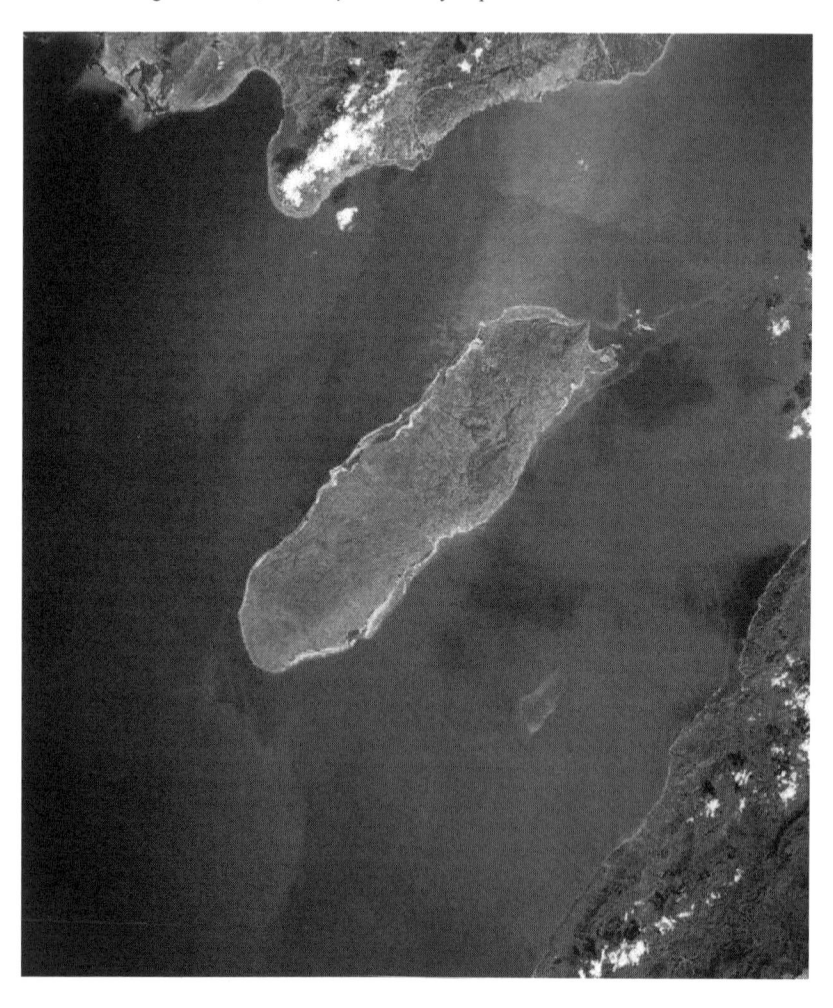

The reef south of the island is the final resting place of the ship.

Chapter 5: The Sea Never Gives Up Its Secrets

"There has never been a clear consensus on any one scenario. It is a mystery that has tormented countless people, including the families of the lost sailors and hundreds of others who have tried in vain to solve the riddle. The Ghost Ship may be the best example of the old proverb that the sea never gives up its secrets." - Brian Hicks, *Ghost Ship* (2004)

As the years passed and nobody ever heard from Briggs or the rest of the passengers on board again, it seemed likely that the story of the *Mary Celeste* would also disappear among the pages of history. Frankly, this might very well have happened, given the wars and economic upheaval that occurred throughout Europe and America during that era.

However, the Victorian Era was a time of growing interest in otherworldly phenomena, and the *Mary Celeste* provided ample fodder for those seeking to make a living by stoking the fires of people's imaginations, among them an ambitious young writer named Arthur Conan Doyle. In January 1884, he wrote a short story, "J. Habakuk Jephson's Statement," that many people construed as an accurate retelling of the story of the ship he called the *Marie Celeste*. In Doyle's tale, a crewman named Jephson survived the ordeal and subsequently described what happened. According to Jephson, he was kidnapped by a madman who killed the others on board and was taken to a strange island: "My statement hitherto may seem so strange as to excite doubt in the minds of those who do not know me, but it was the fact which I am now about to relate which caused my own brother-in-law to insult me by disbelief. I can but relate the occurrence in the simplest words, and trust to chance and time to prove their truth. In the centre of this main street there was a large building, formed in the same primitive way as the others, but towering high above them; a stockade of beautifully polished ebony rails was planted all round it, the framework of the door was formed by two magnificent elephant's tusks sunk in the ground on each side and meeting at the top, and the aperture was closed by a screen of native cloth richly embroidered with gold. We made our way to this imposing looking structure, but, on reaching the opening in the stockade, the multitude stopped and squatted down upon their hams, while I was led through into the enclosure by a few of the chiefs and elders of the tribe, Goring accompanying us, and in fact directing the proceedings. On reaching the screen which closed the temple – for such it evidently was – my hat and my shoes were removed, and I was then led in, a venerable old negro leading the way carrying in his hand my stone, which had been taken from my pocket. The building was only lit up by a few long slits in the roof, through which the tropical sun poured, throwing broad golden bars upon the clay floor, alternating with intervals of darkness."

As was typical of such fiction at the time, the white hero was able to make his escape by fooling the simple natives into believing he was a god. But in the process, Doyle also fooled many of his readers into believing he had finally ferreted out the truth behind the *Mary Celeste*.

Doyle as a young man

Doyle's account helped revive interest in the mystery, but his story was only one of many fictional renditions of the *Mary Celeste* story. In 1913, *The Strand Magazine* published what it billed as a factually accurate account of what happened, given by the only survivor. According to the account, written by someone who identified himself as Fosdyk, everyone but him perished in the ocean when a temporary platform they had rigged fell into the sea. In his fantastic story, the entire complement of the ship save himself gathered on this platform to watch a swimming contest between some of the sailors. When the platform gave way, they were all cast into the ocean and then quickly eaten by sharks.

Although the story was full of errors, many people took it at face value, including a number of newspaper editors from around the country. One of them wrote in January 1914, "In the Strand Magazine appears a remarkable article entitled 'The Marie Celeste. The True Solution of the Mystery.' The story of the Marie Celeste is familiar to most people. It is more than 40 years old and yet no one has been found capable of throwing any light on the fate of the American brig which was found abandoned on the high seas on December 5, 1872, and taken to Gibraltar. No man, woman or child had apparently survived, though there was nothing in the ship to indicate that any particular calamity had happened to her. She was simply abandoned and no member of the ships company was ever heard of again! The story was published in the Strand for August last and readers were invited to send their solutions of that, mystery. Among the letters was one from Mr. A. Howard Linford, headmaster of Peterborough Lodge, England, containing the following paragraph: 'When I read the article the name struck a familiar chord, but it was some days before I could remember under what circumstances I had heard it. At last, however, I recalled an old servant, Abel Fosdyk, committing to my charge, on his death bed, a quantity of papers contained in three boxes; among these he told me would be found the account of (the) 'Mary Celeste.' I suppose he said 'the,' but I had at the time no notion of what Mary Celeste meant, and imagined it was a woman. I paid but little heed, and merely, sent the boxes away to a safe-keeping, not anticipating they would ever be opened again.' Abel Fosdyk was a survivor of the 'Mary Celeste' and in one of the boxes which he left behind was a diary giving a detailed account of what happened to the American brig to cause its being abandoned. The story clears-up a marine mystery which has puzzled the world for more than 42 years."

Other "firsthand accounts" followed, along with a number of speculative accounts. In 1904, one publication insisted that the entire ship's crew was actually picked off the deck by a giant squid. Others speculated that those on board succumbed to some sort of psychic attack, perhaps from the Great Pyramid of Giza or the Bermuda Triangle, which, though hundreds of miles away, was thought to have used its power to perpetrate some sort of crime against the innocent crew.

There have been other nearly as fantastic theories put forth, including the idea that a waterspout travelling across the sea affected the ship's instruments and fooled Briggs into thinking that the ship was sinking when it was actually sound. While it has long been considered possible that faulty instrument readings compelled Briggs to evacuate the ship, one has to wonder why an experienced captain would not wait to get conclusive proof before abandoning ship so suddenly. Similar problems could have been caused by a seaquake, which might have damaged the cargo in its hold and allowed frightening and even deadly fumes to escape.

A 1969 picture of a waterspout

In 2006, an interesting article ran under the provocative title "Solved: The Mystery of the *Mary Celeste.*" The article told readers, "Attention ... focused on the highly volatile cargo. It seemed highly possible that the leaking alcohol caught light, sending Captain Briggs into a panic and prompting the dreaded cry: 'Abandon ship!' It was a plausible explanation but has always been discounted because there was no sign of fire, or explosion. A blast of sufficient magnitude to persuade an experienced captain to take the last resort of abandoning ship would surely have left at least a few scorch marks on the wooden barrels, or in the hold. Now, however, 21st century scientific techniques have been used to finally solve the 19th century mystery. An experiment, conducted by a scientist at UCL for a Channel 5 documentary which will be screened next week, shows that an explosion may indeed be the key to the fate of Captain Briggs, his family and crew. Dr Andrea Sella [UCL Chemistry] built a replica of the hold of the *Mary Celeste*. Using butane gas, he simulated an explosion caused by alcohol leaking from the ship's cargo. Instead of wooden barrels, he used cubes of paper. Setting light to the gas caused a huge blast, which sent a ball of flame upwards. Surely the paper cubes would be burned or blackened or the replica hold damaged. Remarkably, neither happened."

The article went on to quote Dr. Stellas as saying, "What we created was a pressure-wave type of explosion. There was a spectacular wave of flame but, behind it, was relatively cool air. No soot was left behind and there was no burning or scorching. Given all the facts we have, this replicates conditions on board the *Mary Celeste*. The explosion would have been enough to blow open the hatches and would have been completely terrifying for everyone on board. ... It is the most compelling explanation. Of all those suggested, it fits the facts best and explains why they were so keen to get off the ship."

For those who continued to wonder about the fate of the crew and what ultimately happened to them, Paul Begg provided what he believed was a conclusive answer to that issue: "Contrary to the popular imagination, the mystery of *Mary Celeste* is not what happened to her skipper, his family and the crew, since we know that they abandoned ship in the yawl and that the heavily overloaded little boat probably capsized and all aboard were drowned. The mystery is why the crew abandoned a perfectly seaworthy ship. Whatever that something was, it would appear to have happened some time after 8.00 a.m. on Monday, 25 November 1872, and probably quite soon after: up to that time there had been hourly notes on the log slate; there was no cooked food in the galley, no sign of any cooking in preparation or of an interrupted or finished meal; the beds were unmade and the Captain's bed bore the imprint of a child having been asleep there. The weather must have been reasonable because the boat seems to have been launched without the crew attending to the sails, which suggests that there was little more than a light breeze, and this is confirmed by the meteorological records which show that a calm or light wind prevailed that morning. The cabin skylight was also open, which suggests the weather was fair, which is again indicated by the hatch covers being lifted, presumably to air the hold – unless they were lifted after the something that happened. From the evidence provided by the ship herself it is therefore reasonable to deduce that whatever happened was without warning, dramatic and serious enough to greatly alarm an experienced master-mariner and to cause the ship to be abandoned in considerable haste."

In the end, perhaps the most compelling aspect of the *Mary Celeste* is not in any of the findings or evidence but the fact that nearly 150 years later, people are still trying to solve the mystery behind the disappearance of the crew and the young family on board. In his story inspired by the mystery, Arthur Conan Doyle may have put it best when he wrote, "In the utter absence of a clue or grain of evidence, it is to be feared that the fate of the crew of the Marie Celeste will be added to those numerous mysteries of the deep which will never be solved until the great day when the sea shall give up its dead."

The SS Baychimo

Chapter 1: Successful Journeys

Men who spend their lives on sailing ships are inclined to see their vessels as something more than just forms of transportation. Many see them as almost human, referring to them as "her," rather than "it". This is no surprise, since ships do indeed seem to have lives: they are born in dry dock, live lives of leisure or adventure, go to war or play hostess and eventually die, some violently, others by accident or design. Some ships even seem to leave behind a ghost after they are gone, based either in reality or imagination or some combination of both. That is how it was with the *Baychimo*.

A solid ship of iron in the days when this was still considered at least at little novel, she was born in a German port and served in World War I, only to be put up for adoption in the days following the war's end. She was fortunate enough to be adopted into a good and respectable family, the Hudson's Bay Company, and was commanded by good captains and served by well-trained crews. During her short life, she helped open up that Arctic to fur trading, hauling away the furs of delicate animals sacrificed on the altar of commerce and fashion. She also participated in intrepid rescues and even played the part of a spy in an international incident. Along the way she earned a reputation for being one of the best ice ships in the frigid waters off Siberia and Alaska, often getting out of jams that would have sent other vessels into the briny deep.

However, even she could not beat the odds forever, and she finally met her match in the unusually cold winter of 1931. She became trapped in an ice floe she could not get out of and her captain and crew bid her a reluctant goodbye, leaving her to what they assumed to be a quick death between the edges of the crushing ice.

As fate would have it, the *Baychimo*'s journey did not end when her crew left. Instead, she was to play a new role in the Arctic, rising like a frozen Phoenix out of ice instead of fire to sail again for years as a mysterious ghost ship rarely seen but often spoken of. Because of the decades that she remained afloat without any human hand to guide her, her story in both life and death remains one of the most mysterious tales of the Arctic's frozen seas.

In 1991, journalist David Gunston introduced his readers to the ship's largely forgotten story, writing for *UNESCO Courier*, "ONE of the world's strangest sea stories is still unfinished, and looks like remaining so for a long time, perhaps forever. This is the story of the Baychimo, the deserted ghost ship that refuses to die and still haunts human memory and curiosity." He went on to describe the fate of a ship that, for more than a half century, sailed around the Arctic completely unmanned, her only captain the ice floes that determined her course, her only crew the currents that carried her where they led.

While the world may have mostly forgotten the *Baychimo* by the 1990s, there was a time when she was new. The ship was launched in 1915 at the Lindholmens shipyard in Sweden. Weighing in at over 1,300 tons, the 230 foot craft made her maiden voyage that year to Hamburg, Germany under the power of a triple expansion steam engine. During World War I, she served the German Kaiser, specializing in making her way through icy waters. Germany lost the war and under the terms of the Treaty of Versailles, "Germany recognizes the right of the Allied and Associated Powers to the replacement, ton for ton (gross tonnage) and class for class, of all merchant ships and fishing boats lost or damaged owing to the war."

As a result, the ship was declared part of those reparations and was sent to Great Britain in 1920, where she was bought up by the Hudson's Bay Company. Originally called *Ångermanelfven*, she was renamed *Baychimo*. Baychimo was first captained by Thomas Smellie, an Englishman. Smellie, an experienced captain, assumed the helm of the Baychimo at the age of 41. On June 21st, the Baychimo left St.Nazaire, France, on its way across the Atlantic.

Upon arriving in Montreal, Smellie turned the ship over to Captain Enoch Falk for use in the Arctic. July 16 saw her set sail with a cargo of supplies needed to establish a company headquarters in one of the coldest parts of the world. She arrived in Pond Inlet before the end of summer and dropped off 175 tons of cargo. She then left there on September 1 and set sail to find another port from which the company could also operate. They finally settled on Pangnirtung Fjord.

Soon, the *Baychimo* was on her way back to England via Montreal, her career in the Arctic off to a flying start. In the following year she sailed along the coast of Siberia under Captain Bertram Edmunds, who said of her, "She is really a wonderful vessel in heavy weather and I have no fear for any storms we may encounter in the future. Like all low-powered vessels she naturally does not make much headway against high head seas, but she certainly does at least as well as many larger vessels and certainly behaves much better."

He also spoke well of his crew, though not so much of the coal engines used to power the vessel: "If you could see your staff from Captain down absolutely black from head to foot almost every day you would be surprised how people work and how happy they remain. If it were not for the willing manner in which your officers work the keeping of the bunkers supplied would indeed be a problem. … During the voyage we have shifted about 600 tons of coal. 400 from No. 3 hold and 200 from No. 2. If you can imagine wheeling a barrow full of coal along a rolling switch-back railway and forcing a 2' 10" basket through a 2' 9" space you will be able to appreciate some of the difficulties we have had to contend with and will understand how it is we have not shifted more of the coal from No. 2…."

Chapter 2: A Change of Luck

In early July 1922, the *Baychimo* experienced its first serious problem, running aground near Olyutorka on the Russian Coast. In order to lighten her load sufficiently to get away, she had to offload more than $50,000 worth of merchandise, including

> "750 sheets of corrugated iron
>
> 6 sacks of rice
>
> 4 cases of kerosene

94 cases of gasoline

6 barrels of salt beef

94 cases of sapporo beer

9 bales of grey dill [cloth]

1 case of necklaces

18 barrels of pickled cabbage

3 bales of grass rope

317½ dozen cups and saucers

78 dozen wash basins

20 dozen chamber pots

2 dozen buckets"

Finally free, the ship continued her trading mission up and down the Siberian coast. Then, as winter approached, the men of the *Baychimo* happily turned toward home, making their way south along the American West Coast and through the Panama Canal.

After a stop at Norfolk, Virginia, they began their Atlantic crossing in late December, only to run into very bad weather. The ship's December 29 log read, "4:00 AM Hard westerly gale. High mountainous sea. Violent squalls of hale and snow. Hurricane force. Vessel labouring and straining heavily and shipping heavy water fore and aft. Engines violently racing. ... [2:20 PM] Vessel running before hard gale as above. Shipped heavy sea over the stern and the following damage was done. Awning spars washed away and stanchions bent out of place. Star[board]lifeboat pushed out of position and chocks washed overboard, also the two lifebuoys off after rail on boat deck. After bulkhead of engine room house buckled in, at the same time cracking the bracket holding the steering barrel. Interior of 2nd Engineer's room sprung out of position. After WC door and frame again washed away. It is feared that other fractures and strains will be found in the vicinity of the damage when same is overhauled for repairs. One complete Walker's Cherub Log [which measured distance travelled through the water] washed away from rail."

The ship finally made it to England, and made dry dock repairs. In the past few years, the Baychimo had suffered much ice damage from its Artic journeys.

For his part, Edmunds had had enough and refused to return to the Arctic in February, writing to the company, "I regret to say I feel unable to take command again and consequently must resign from my position as master. This is the first time during nineteen years in command that I ever gave up an appointment & I only do so now because what is demanded of me is unreasonable & any practical seaman knows it is so."

He was replaced by Captain Sydney Cromwell, of whom one of his men wrote, "Our Captain, short, rotund, with a reddish face, clean-shaven and with little bits of scanty hair. A man from Kent, born to the sea, a bull-doggish type, aloof, not to be crossed if one can avoid it, a small man who has to stretch his arms to hold the binoculars over the canvas windscreen of the bridge, with fat hands almost childlike emerging from the gilt cuffs of his jacket; a man with an unimpressive flat tenor voice, sometimes petulant, peevish, sometimes unexpectedly good-humoured, but most often, to the fo'c'sle, hard and indifferent."

Cromwell's instructions were clear: he was manage his ship as he saw best but was not to think of himself as completely independent. The company insisted:

> "The special nature of the Kamchatka trade, however, makes it necessary that one of the Company's Superintending Officers, together with two or more assistants, should accompany the steamer, and we require you to follow his (Superintending Officer) instructions in regard to:
>
> "1 The order of calling of your vessel at the various ports in the itinerary attached hereto.
>
> "2 The stowage of your cargo in the various holds and on deck—always excepting that the question of the trim of the vessel is a matter for which you are responsible.
>
> "3 The co-operation of the crew in working the cargo whilst in port.
>
> "4 The disposition of the passenger accommodation other than that required for officers and crew, and we rely upon you to assist the Superintendent to the very best of your ability, bearing in mind that the sole purpose of your steamer is to facilitate the trade under the instructions of the Superintendent."

The *Baychimo* set sail from England on February 14, 1923 and again ran into bad weather, with Cromwell recording:

> "Feb. 16: Shipped heavy sea fore well deck, damaging steam pipes and casing leading to windlass.
>
> "Feb. 18: All forecastle ports stove in and three port frames damaged. Shipped

heavy seas over mid-ship house shifting starboard life-boat and both small boats, damaging boat chocks and boat covers torn beyond repair. Feb. 19: Shipped heavy sea forward breaking down starboard spars and twisting stanchions and starboard rail at forecastle head out of proportion. Pooped [by a] heavy sea moving iron wheel-box out of position and bending struts. Steward's storeroom port stove in. Port frame bent."

Toward the end of their voyage, *Baychimo* once again became caught up in an unusual situation involving a dispute between the United States and a new adversary, the Soviet Union. On July 27, 1923, the *Associated Press* reported, "Officers and crew of the American trading schooner Iskum of Tacoma, Wash., were being congratulated here today on having freed themselves from the custody of the soviet government of Russia. Owners of the craft had been informed that trade with Russian countries was carried on at the risk of the trader and that therefore the American state department could do nothing to help. In this dilemma the men of the Iskum seized soviet guards placed aboard their vessels to keep the craft in Siberian waters, put the custodians in irons, made an escape from Anadyr and crossed the Bering Sea to Nome. Today the Iskum which belongs to the Phoenix Northern Trading company of Tacoma was lying here and the erstwhile guards were in the custody of American authorities. Much comment was heard about the part played by a Hudson's Bay trading vessel, the Baychimo, in the escape of the Iskum. Ordered to prevent the Iskum from getting away, the Baychimo ran aground, though the soviet authorities had been reported friendly to the Hudson's Bay company and inimical to the Americans. It was said that someone aboard the Baychimo had put her steering gear out of order. After leaving Anadyr, the Iskum which was one of four American schooners that the soviet authorities at East Cape, Siberia, ordered held on charges of violating Russian trading laws, made for St. Lawrence Island, an American possession in the Bering Sea."

After a successful summer trading and establishing new Hudson's Bay Company outposts, not to mention helping American prisoners escape, the *Baychimo* pulled into port in Vancouver on November 2 to find a letter waiting concerning her return trip to England. It seems that the company was concerned about maximizing space for both the coal needed to run the ship and the cargo needed to fund it. Cromwell was told, "In order to try and avoid carrying coal on deck, we have decided to load the cargo before bunkering at Comox, so as to enable you to have as much space as possible in the after 'tween decks [the hold]. It will be necessary, however, to see that the after 'tween deck hatches and the trimming hatches are well corked and tarpaulins securely battened down so that no question whatsoever may arise regarding damage to cargo by coal dust. We look to you to give this matter your personal attention."

Another problem soon rose to plague the company: the *Baychimo* was kept from returning home by a dock workers' strike. Cromwell wrote in dismay, "The expenses for loading [have] been much higher than expected. This was on account of having to work on a Sunday and the Monday being a general holiday. If I had not agreed to work these days I should have lost my turn for the berth, which would have been another four to five days delay." At the same time, his ship was carrying a prize load of furs and other items: "18,611 Viporotki [white fox] skins in 264 packages, 95 polar bear skins in 20 packages, 2,592 lbs of whalebone, plus the skins of 50 hair seals, 50 spotted seals, 25 parchment seals, 2 walrus and 2 laktak [bearded seal] in an additional 6 packages."

Baychimo's 1924 voyage was interrupted when she was called up to help another ship with whom she would eventually share a similar fate. The *Lady Kindersley* was a cargo ship that became stuck in ice in early August. Unable to get her loose, her crew abandoned her on August 31. The *Canadian Press* reported on September 3, "An effort is to he made to salvage the $400,000 cargo of the gasoline schooner Lady Kindersley of Vancouver, whose crew abandoned her in the ice of the Arctic ocean Sunday, 50 miles from Point Barrow, Alaska, the Hudson Bay company, owner, announced today. The Kindersley's crew was rescued by the steamer Boxer of the United States bureau of education. The Baychimo, another vessel of the company, which had been dispatched to the aid of the Kindersley, arrived Sunday in the vicinity of the Boxer, C. H. French of this city, manager of the company's fur trade department, was advised. He ordered the Baychimo to try to reach the side of the Kindersley, which was abandoned three miles from the Boxer. No report since that of Sunday has come from the Boxer, which was to have gone to Nome, Alaska, with the crews of the Kindersley and of the Arctic of San Francisco, which was abandoned last month in the same vicinity."

Unfortunately, the *Baychimo* was not able to salvage the cargo before the ship went down. " The Kindersley gallantly tried to rescue the Baychimo for days, but inclement weather finally forced them to turn back.

1925 saw the *Baychimo* make her first voyage to the Central Arctic, northeast of Alaska. To make matters unnecessarily difficult, Cromwell was informed that a number of company executives would be joining him for the trip, and that they would be taking over the quarters normally assigned to him and his crew. A note warned, "We wish everyone to feel that the Company's steamers are operated by men imbued with a desire to give cheerful and willing help to all with whom they come in contact. We are sure you can help us greatly in this respect."

The men on board during this trip got more than they bargained for when they witnessed the horrific site of a pod of orcas attacking another whale. The young deck boy, Donald Gillingham, wrote, "An upsurge of water five cable-lengths from us on the starboard bow brought me to the alert; a black shape rose up, fluked at the end, a huge Excalibur, and slowly swung over, hitting the sea with a geysered smash of spray; as it did so, some black-and-white lesser shapes appeared darting around it—killer whales, the wolves of the sea. They leapt out of the water and came down on the back of the Bowhead Whale, striving to stun it, and others were doubtless attacking from beneath...."

As it turned out, this excitement was merely peremptory to the real crisis that soon faced the crew in September 1925, when the *Baychimo's* luck finally ran out. The ship continued its journey and in mid-August, Cromwell reported to the company, "We arrived [Cambridge Bay] 8:15 PM, considerable delay was caused there through gale of wind, ship drifting with two anchors down and with great difficulty we just managed to keep ship clear of the beach." A crew member was a bit more emotional and explained, "We were going full speed ahead with both our anchors out. With our anchors and screw we fought the hurricane in that remote and shelterless bay in Victoria Island, but even so our stern touched. We could feel the sudden grip, a hand from the dead. A flash [of light] disclosed the beach—from where I was it looked under the counter. Then the anchors got a hold ... and the winch ... pulled us free."

Then, a few days later, disaster struck. The *Associated Press* reported on September 12, "The steamer Baychimo of the Hudson's Bay company, trading out Vancouver, B.C., which last month was punctured by ice in the Arctic ocean, was reported by radio today frozen fast and crying for help. The Baychimo was reported in the report to be off Herschel Island. Mariners here accustomed to the Arctic, stated that, there was no possibility that any boat could go to the rescue of the Baychimo, but that her men, even if she was in considerable distance from shore, had a good chance to reach land over the ice. The previous report on the Baychimo was: 'Had starboard side stove in by left for distance of twenty feet and was leaking eight feet dally.'"

A few days later, on September 17, the *Helena (Montana) Independent* put a personal spin on the story: "Two Kalispell men, Lyman and Gus DeStaffany, are aboard the S. S. Baychimo, reported Saturday by The Associated Press to be frozen fast in the Arctic ocean and calling for help. A message received here Sunday by their brother, James DeStaffany, gave the information that the ship was not yet frozen in, but that she was in danger of such a fate. The message, which is believed to have been sent from the ship by radio to Cordova, Alaska, Saturday, by wireless from there to Seattle, and by telegram to Kalispell, read: "Aboard Baychimo. May get frozen in Arctic and travel overland. Lyman." After five years of trapping and trading in furs in the Coronation Gulf country, about 1,000 miles east of Hersehel island, the two brothers started home last spring. They went into the north after being discharged from the army. Gus came home to Kalispell two years ago, and on his return had a schooner made in Vancouver, traveling by way of the MacKenzie river to the Arctic ocean. They are coming out for good this time, according to a letter written in December."

Then, just when the men seemed almost resigned to a winter on the ice, their luck changed and they found a chance to get out of their predicament. The story came out on October 2: "Word has been received by wireless via Cordova and Seattle that the Hudson's Bay company steamship Baychlmo is making an effort to come out from the Arctic and, according to Captain Sydney Cornwall, has a good chance to do so. The ship was at Tangent Point about 50 miles east of Point Barrow at 8 o'clock Thursday night and if she rounds Point-Barrow she will be able to get clear of ice, it's said. Apparently the hole in her hull has been sufficiently patched. The message from Capt. Cornwall said: "Off Tangent- Point and prospects good for rounding Point Barrow."

Indeed, their prospects turned out to be better than good, and they did break free. On October 5, the *Canadian Press* reported, "The Hudson's Bay steamer Baychimo, caught in the Arctic ice floes in August, has fought her way out and Is now en route to Unalaska to bunker, according to a wireless message received by the company officials today. After taking on fuel it is expected the vessel will reach Vancouver within twenty days."

Once they were back in Vancouver, the crew had quite a story to tell, and on November 25, the wire services reported, "Fog mirages, faulty soundings and stormy weather played cruel tricks with the Hudson's Bay company trading vessel Baychimo during its long voyage in the Arctic, and it was only through a strange turn of fate that she was able to-for woodcock, hut reach here safely after being imprisoned for twenty-nine days in the ice off Herschell Island. After being caught in the ice late August, twelve attempts were made to buck the heavy fields without success. The strongest gales roaring down out of the north, failed to break up or shift the huge pack and the Baychimo was helpless in its grip. Several times the vessel worked its way clear of the floes only to be held back after a few hours and locked in a more powerful grip than before. Finally it was decided to prepare the ship for a winter in the Arctic. On September 20, however, some members of the crew who had landed at Herschel Island, reported having seen clear water. The following day the Baychimo made another break for the open and succeeded in crashing through. Fog, however, which had settled on the water for days, lifted and open water was seen ahead without a trace of ice. The vessel ploughed ahead over the Arctic seas for four days and nights. Then the unexpected happened. The weather suddenly turned colder. Snow-laden gusts of wind drove across the Baychimo's bows. At night an ice 'blink' or reflection from the sky was visible. A solid wall of ice suddenly loomed ahead, stretching for miles and towering fourteen feet high, an unbroken stretch of ice—the Polar pack. 'Full astern' was ordered and the ship, in the nick of time, backed away. Had she hit, her bows would have been crumpled like an egg-shell and the ship and crew would have gone to the bottom. It was concluded that the soundings had been misleading; that the Baychimo was lost. But at daybreak Captain S. A. Cornwall saw through the haze what appeared to be a church steeple. He doubted his own vision at first. They he heard the yelping of dogs. A miracle had brought the little trading vessel out of the Arctic wilderness to the village of Point Barrow, which was then rounded and the vessel headed for Dutch Harbor, Alaska, to replenish her fuel supply to carry her to Vancouver."

Chapter 3: Final Voyages

Following this great adventure, the *Baychimo* continued to make her annual round trip voyages from England to the Northern Arctic and back. These trips were especially hard on the men, as crew members were not allowed to leave the ship, even when it called in ports. According to the company manual, "Whenever the steamer is anchored off any of the Company's posts during the course of the voyage, no member or members of the crew except for the Ice Pilot must be allowed on shore on 'leave' nor must any member or members of the crew be allowed to remain on shore [after unloading] unless it is absolutely necessary, and an entry should be made in the

Log Book of any exception."

That is not to say that there were no diversions, or that the men had no unique experiences while serving on the *Baychimo*. For instance, in 1926 they were part of a new breakthrough in communications. According to one wire service article, "A 1200-mile radio telephone conversation in the arctic, said to be the longest ever made in that region, was reported by the trading steamer Baychimo, which arrived here today with furs valued at $250,000. The radio operator of the Baychimo said he established telephone communication with the steamship Bay Rupert on two nights in July. The Baychimo was in the western Canadian arctic, while the Bay Rupert was near the northern entrance of Hudson's Bay."

While there were no doubt many adventures, most of them were never recorded or have been lost in the annals of time. Most days, the sailors busied themselves with the tasks necessary to get their ship and its cargo from one place to the next safely. This was an exciting time in the history of fur trading, as *London's Contemporary Review* noted: "The most romantic story of all regarding quick fortunes made in the 'booming Arctic' is that of the two DeStaffany brothers. Five years ago these two trappers from Montana penetrated the Arctic by way of Edmonton and the Mackenzie river route. They had less than £40 between them. In the autumn of 1925 they came out of the Arctic on the Hudson's Bay company's steamer Baychimo with furs which they sold for £20,000. Undoubtedly the Arctic boom will increase when such fortunes lie ready for the making. The trapping regulations are not severe. American trading vessels are not allowed to trade in these Canadian Arctic waters beyond Herschel Island. But an independent American can get a special permit to trap on Canadian soil. The same applies to men of other countries. Any foreigner, by becoming a naturalized Canadian, may take a trading vessel into these western Arctic sea, providing the ship Is entered under Canadian articles. A Canadian subject may trap without license, but is required to pay 4 shillings for every white fox skin taken. For white skins the traders give such things as flour, tobacco, tea, sugar, milk, fancy biscuits, white man's clothes, pots and pans, guns, ammunition, blankets, steel spearheads, hooks and knives, and many other things both useful and useless. Gramophones are in great demand and command a high price. Telescopes are much prized by the Eskimos, and a cheap pair of field glasses sometimes sells for as much an £15."

What the article failed to mention was that the *Baychimo* was responsible for both bringing trade goods in and taking furs out of the Arctic. In this way, her cargo hold was rarely empty.

Of course, sometimes their cargo was livelier than others, as the *Manitoba Free Press* reported in July 1927: "Having completed nearly 1,000 miles of a 3,000-mile journey, a team of eight husky dogs have arrived here from a point near Armstrong, in northern Ontario. They are bound for Coronation gulf in the Arctic. They will embark on the steamship Baychimo, which sails Thursday. The dogs are consigned to the Inspector of the Hudson's Bay company at Coronation Gulf and are a specially trained team developed for stamina, and long distance pulls."

The few records that remain tell the story of a captain and crew consumed with the daily toil of life in the harsh Arctic. Consider this excerpt from 1928:

> "August 20th. 5:00 AM Resumed loading of ballast, moderate breeze. At 1:00 PM anchor aweigh and proceeded on voyage to Flagstaff Island. At 9:35 PM anchored in 14 fathoms off White Bear Point [located about two-thirds of the way to Flagstaff Island].
>
> "Aug 21st at 3:00 AM weighed anchor and proceeded, fresh breeze and hazy weather. At 7:00 AM anchored in 13 fathoms in dense fog. 8:45 AM weather cleared. Weighed anchor and proceeded. Light winds and fog banks. 1:45 PM anchored off Flagstaff Island. From Cambridge Bay to the anchorage there seems to be good water when well clear of the land, but along the shore the islands and reefs run out a good many miles. Commenced discharging on arrival. At 9:00 PM launch and lighter left ship for outpost, which is about 12 miles away, for some freight and natives.
>
> "Aug 22nd. At 7:00 AM launch and lighter returned and brought back freight, natives and their effects. 4:00 PM all cargo discharged. Light and launch lifted anchor weighed and proceeded voyage at 5:15 PM."

As time went on and the *Baychimo* demonstrated an ability to go where few other ships could survive and to maneuver through some of the coldest and most difficult parts of the world, the Hudson's Bay Company demanded more and more from both the ship and her crew. In the summer of 1930, Cromwell received the following orders: "You will proceed from Vancouver with the Western Arctic supplies as usual, clear up all your work as far as Cambridge Bay, arriving there at the earliest possible moment. So far as Cambridge Bay the route is known to you, and from Cambridge Bay to King William Land [that is, King William Island] you will be preceded by the M.S. Fort Macpherson. From King William Land outwards the route is via Rae Strait, keeping well to the eastward of Matty Island, thence through or around Spence Bay to Boothia Peninsula and close up along that coast. By the time you reach Peterson Bay, King William Land, say 20th August, the M.S. Fort James should be in Lancaster Sound on her homeward journey, so that every part of your route will be reported upon before you start out on it."

Proud of his crew and their record, Cromwell replied simply, "I am confident that we can make the Northwest passage unless there is exceptional ice conditions to be met. This can only be decided about by seeing the ice for yourself as what would stop a small boat would not prevent the Baychimo from getting through ... I trust the proposed venture will be carried out in the 1930 Season."

Soon the ship was on her way again, her one towering funnel a familiar sight in Arctic waters.

She made her usual run, delivering food and supplies to the Eskimo villages and picking up that year's haul of furs to be sold in England. Cromwell and his crew returned home that winter and prepared to make the next trip, unaware that it would be their last aboard the *Baychimo*.

Chapter 4: 1931

Somewhat fittingly, the 1931 trip got off to a bad start for *Baychimo*, as Anthony Dalton, author of *Baychimo: Arctic Ghost Ship* pointed out: "Baychimo's registered capacity for passengers and crew was 40 persons, the maximum number that could safely be carried in her lifeboats. The steamer already had a cargo certificate issued by Canadian authorities. In 1931 a government inspector suggested the ship should have a passenger certificate as well. He let Cornwell know he was well aware that the ship had, on occasions, carried more than 40 people, and warned him of the possibility of a heavy fine if he was caught. ... Ever mindful of the profit motive, the Company's reply emphatically refused to entertain the idea of obtaining a Passenger Certificate, as that would inevitably create additional expenses to alter the ship's accommodation structure."

Cromwell passed the warning on to the Hudson's Bay Company, adding, "Previous years we have had as many as eighty persons aboard on the passage between some of the posts and I expect it will be the same this season."

In reply to his request for their help, the company wrote back, "The ship is in a very special trade and generally the persons we carry above the crew are Government officials, Church of England and Roman Catholic Missionaries and Hudson's Bay officials. May I suggest, could it not be possible to get a special permit from the Government at Ottawa to carry on with this kind of trade? ... We suggest that the difficulty might be overcome by putting the passengers on Articles at the nominal [1 shilling] per month. We appreciate your efforts to facilitate the Company's business and will leave it to your discretion to deal with matters as they arise during your voyage."

Unfortunately, Cromwell had already tried that, so he wrote back, "The Canadian Inspectors here know that we have been signing passengers on the Articles at 1 [shilling] per month and they told me it was not lawful to do same."

Nevertheless, the company insisted it remained his problem to solve, and ultimately, the *Baychimo* went back out as usual, crossing the Atlantic in the spring of 1931 and putting in at Vancouver for supplies and fuel before heading out again on July 7. On March 1, The *Charleston (West Virginia) Daily Mail* ran a story written by someone who had spent time in the Arctic: "I felt in all the people of Coppermine that sense of waiting. The arrival of the Baychimo is the great event of the year. She brings coal (which here costs $87 a ton) and canned food; blankets and furniture and other supplies; the year's mail— and new faces. She sets out from Vancouver early in July, and there is always the fear that perhaps she won't be able to round Point Barrow in season to get as far as Cambridge Bay, the end of the journey. She is due about the middle of August, and for days before she comes people don't trouble to go to bed—though, as the sun shines for twenty-four hours, sleeping time is a matter of choice. It is a wonderful moment when the Baychimo steams into the harbor, every inch of space taken, canoes even hung amid the rigging. The Hudson's Bay Company has been going since 1920 and it does not fail people. It is said that no explorer can suffer in the North now, for a Hudson's Bay post is sure to be within reach. No chance traveler is ever refused a welcome."

In 1931, however, the crew soon ran into worse than usual weather. On July 30, Cromwell recorded, "Moderate to whole gale from S.W., rough to high sea. Engines used to ease strain on anchor. 90 fathm. out. Ice being tightly packed to the shore." The next day, he wrote, "Moderate to strong W.N.W. gale, rough sea, overcast and squally weather. 4:45 PM hove up anchor and proceeded close to edge of ice. No leads could be seen, ice tightly packed to shore. Proceeded to anchorage and at 6:25 PM anchored about 4 miles off-shore in 10 fathoms of water. Ice pack moving slowly to Northward."

Things only got worse as the trip progressed, as these log entries show:

> "30th August. 3:50 AM Weather cleared; light easterly winds. Hove up anchor and proceeded eastwards, vessel working through heavy pans and scattered ice from one lead to another. Propeller striking the ice very heavily at times. 10:00 AM Moderate easterly breeze and ice loosening up with occasional patches of fog. After following a lead a considerable distance in the fog it came to an end: dense fog set in and stopped the vessel. 1:00 PM Weather cleared and proceeded through very heavy pans and close drift ice for about 4 miles to gain a more open lead. Ship backing and filling and breaking heavy pans up to get by, the propeller striking the ice heavily at times. 3:30 PM gained more open leads. 6:00 PM to 8:30 PM working ship through very heavy pans and closely packed drift ice to gain more open lead towards Baillie Island."

> "31st August. 0:50 AM Anchored in 5 fathoms of water owing to dense fog. 4:00 AM weather cleared and proceeded, working ship through heavy pans and scattered ice. 8:05 AM Pullen Island abeam, about 6 miles off. Noon. Moderate E.N.E. wind and open water. 5:30 PM passed Cape Dalhousie about 4 miles off."

And yet, as Gunston later explained, "Day and night, under the misty glow of the never setting sun, the Baychimo steamed on eastward. Eventually they reached the end of their normal eastward run by the shores of Victoria Island. With the hold crammed with cargo, the relieved captain turned the Baychimo about for Vancouver. Unfortunately winter came early that year to this bleak northern wasteland. Ferocious winds and deep-freezing conditions brought the dreaded pack-ice south much quicker than usual. By 30 September only a narrow stretch of open water remained for the ship to steam through, and on 1 October the ice closed in. Her engines at stop, she could only move as the creaking ice willed. She was not far from the Alaskan village of Barrow, where the company had permanent huts built ashore. Seeing that a terrible blizzard was imminent, Cornwell ordered his men to trudge across the kilometre or so of ice to shelter in these huts, where they remained for two days, half-frozen and unable to venture out."

Then, the ice broke away as quickly as it had formed and the men rushed back to their ship and went again on their way, only to become stuck again a few hours later. This time, they were stuck for good and began to make themselves at home on their new frozen property. At this point, they had enough food and fuel to survive; if anything, the main threat was boredom, one they coped with by organizing active football games.

Then, on October 8, right in the middle of a match, the men heard a sound they dreaded: the loud cracking noise of the ice they were cased in breaking away from the rest of the larger ice floe. The crack moved quickly across the very area where they were playing, and soon the ship, still held solid in its frozen cocoon, was floating toward land and possible destruction.

Cornwell radioed for help but still refused to abandon his ship. On October 10, the *Associated Press* reported, "Practically all hopes have been given up of the Baychimo getting out of the ice. Continuous southerly winds have packed the ice in solid for miles around the ship. The first southerly gale will bring a movement of heavy ice which will either carry the ship on the beach or crush, it. Some passengers have been taken by dog team to Wainwright and are to spend the winter there, while others are to fly to Nome and make connections with the last Victoria. It is understood airplanes have been contracted for. Preparations have been made to build a suitable house on the beach near the vessel for the use of the crew this winter."

A few days later, on October 15, the *Associated Press* updated its readers on the situation in the far northwest, explaining, "Three Northern Air Transport planes are taking off for the Baychimo, icebound near Wainwright, today to bring out from 12 to 15 passengers. Pilot Chester Brown, Hans Mirow and Vic Roes are making the trip. They are taking a ton of supplies from here for the crew of the Baychimo, which will winter at the boat." The planes airlifted the ship's passengers and about half its crew, leaving the rest behind to care for the ship and her expensive cargo.

An October 21 article explained: "Seventeen men, the captain and the crew of the ice-locked ship Baychimo, fear a long and hazardous winter far north of the Arctic circle while the Baychimo's passengers, 'rescued' by airplanes, are far away to the south. In a hastily built winter house on the beach the men will spend the eight or nine months until the sun again melts the ice in the far north. No village lies within 30 miles. The plight of the little band, commanded by Capt. S. A. Cornwall of London, was described today by passengers brought out by airplane. The passengers will sail for the south soon on the last ship of the season to leave here. 'We are surely glad to arrive at home.' H. G. Bonnycastle of Winnipeg said, on stepping from the plane a w eek after having: left the Baychimo. 'These fliers did great work, over hazardous flying country and in Arctic conditions.' He referred to pilots Vie Ross and Hana Mirow of the Northern Air Transport company, who began the rescue work soon after all hope was given up of freeing the Baychimo. It was caught in the ice shortly after leaving Point Barrow, several week s ago. Bonnycastle said the Baychimo, a Hudson Bay Company trading ship, rests about a quarter mile from shore. She has a chance to winter through, members of the crew believe, if the shore ice does not move or she is not crushed by incoming floes. In addition to Bonnycastle, six other Canadian passengers arrived here yesterday."

A picture of the Nascopie (on the right) arriving to help the crew

Indeed, the *Baychimo* was gone, and all that remained was a mountain of ice nearly 100 feet tall. The *Associated Press* reported on December 1: "The treacherous Arctic ice pack, quiet after a three day storm, today held the secret of the disappearance of the vessel Baychimo, lost in the shifting ice. Whether ground to pieces and sunk, where it had been frozen in for two months some 60 miles south of here or carried away to sea by the moving floes, was not known by the five members of the crew who had been living in winter quarters on shore. A high ridge in the ice pack, where the vessel had been resting, remained, the crew reported in a message received here last night, but no trace of the wreckage could be found. A search team 10 miles from shore on the ice, and to the north and south, failed to reveal any signs of the steel hulled vessel."

With nothing left to do, the crew returned to the mainland and began making plans to get back home, thinking that their ship and her cargo likely lay at the bottom of the frigid sea. However, they soon learned they were wrong. Just a few days later, a man who had been out hunting saw the ship drifting along and rushed back to tell Cornwell. He quickly organized a party to go see if the man's report was true and discovered it was. The *Baychimo* was now a ghost ship, piloted by unseen forces like currents and ice floes. Even as the men stood looking at their former home, they felt certain that they could never pilot it out of the sea of ice that was surrounding it. They boarded her one last time, rescued as many of the most valuable furs that they could carry and said good bye to their vessel for the last time. They all agreed that the ship had only days or maybe weeks left before it collided with something large enough to take her down.

Two years later, on October 22, 1933, a newspaper story recounted the tale: "When the steamship became locked in the ice a year ago, Captain Sidney A. Cornwall and a few members of the crew built a crude shack on the shore a mile or more over the frozen wastes from the vessel. They packed the snow tight about its rough walls to keep out the elements. They made stoves out of the oil drums taken from the ship, so that they could keep warm. And when airplanes took the other members of the crew and effects of the Hudson's Bay company south to Nome, they settled down to await the distant coming of spring, when the ice would break up and the Baychimo would be free to proceed south again. It meant waiting through the long, cold, dark Arctic winter, but Cornwall and his men were ready for the ordeal. So they lived subsisting on canned goods and reindeer meat supplied by friendly Eskimos. Each day two or more of their number trudged out to the steamship to keep the propeller free of ice. It had to be done, no matter how cold the weather or how biting the winter gale. If not, the Baychimo would be a crippled ship unable to navigate when the spring thaw came. All went well until Christmas Eve. That night the temperature rose suddenly from 60 degrees below zero to 1C degrees above, and a fierce gale began blowing from the southwest. The little shack which was home to Captain Cornwall and his men vibrated constantly. It seemed as though it would be blown to pieces any minute by the terrific wind. Outside one could not see one's hand before one's face, so wild were the elements. But then, one did not venture out. It was not safe to do so. For three days the storm lasted. The open water, out beyond the Baychimo, rose six feet and more, and the Ice crushed in toward the shore, piling up ridges fifty to seventy feet in height. And then toward noon of the third nay the storm abated. Peering out from the shack, the men could only see mountainous ridges of ice where the Baychimo had been. By 3 o'clock in the afternoon, the weather was such that they could go outside, and when they did so they found that the Baychimo had vanished."

Chapter 5: The Ghost Ship

While the *Baychimo* was gone, it was far from forgotten. A group of travelers, including Charlie Adraigailak and Ollie Morris, encountered the Baychimo near Point Barrow, Alaska. The men went aboard and found a cargo of furs.

When word spread that there was a ship full of priceless furs floating around the Arctic, treasure hunters and other adventurers quickly took notice. On January 14, 1932, the *Associated Press* reported, "A lost treasure of furs, valued at $1,500,000 will be sought by William B. Graham, Alaska filer…. Graham said he will use his specially constructed plane in a search for the steamer Baychimo, frozen fast in the Arctic ice somewhere south of Point Barrow. The flier said the ship was abandoned by the Hudson Bay Fur company when It became icebound, and he intends to exercise salvage rights—if he can find it."

Others had similar ideas, with a January 19 article reporting, "Night flying in the frozen Arctic circle in search of the missing vessel Baychimo, Hudson's Bay company fur ship, and then flying fur pelts valued at $1,000,000 from the ship to shore, was the huge undertaking cut out today for Don Graham, 35, Alaskan airmail pilot. Graham, here en route to Point Barrow, Alaska, will fly over the Arctic Ocean south in search for the vessel which disappeared early last fall. ... Graham will fly a six-place cabin plane. Special equipment will include a powerful spot-landing light, which he said was expected to illuminate a large area from altitudes up to 2000 feet. 'The area in which the ship was lost,' he said, is the graveyard for fur ships and if the Baychimo survives the winter, she may be 'enveloped by the ice when it piles up during the spring thaw.'"

There is no way to know for certain how many pilots flew up and down the Alaskan coast looking for the lost ship, but none ever found it. Instead, the vessel took up the habit of showing up where it was least expected, appearing before people not even looking for it. The October 22, 1933 story recalled, "Airplanes were used to hunt for the missing ship and finally, after many weeks, she was sighted, twisted like putty and with a long gap in her sides, but not yet in Davy Jones' locker. Fourteen bales of furs were recovered from her hold before she vanished again. Then weeks passed without another sign of this Flying Dutchman of the North. It appeared certain that she had gone to the bottom. But no! There came a day in spring when the ice commenced to break up. Out in the open water, five miles offshore, a group of Eskimos were fishing. And while they fished, there came a sudden cracking of the ice. It began to move as the wind opened up leads, and while the Eskimos watched in amazement, a vessel—the Baychimo—rose like a ghost out of the deep gullies in the pack and drifted toward them. But, like a phantom ship, it was gone again before the natives had time to reach shore, report their discovery and bring white men back to the spot."

On March 12, 1932, Leslie Melvin, then a young trapper traveling between Herschel Island and Nome, spotted the soon to be mystical ship. In 1936, he described the encounter: "I wouldn't make another effort [to] board the Baychimo even if could locate her. By this time she has been completely gutted of everything her crew left aboard. ... The Baychimo was listed over on her port side resting on top of the ice when I first reached her. It was no trick to scramble to her deck as the sailors had left a ladder hanging over the side. Although the Baychimo had hardly become a true ghost ship at that time, it was plenty spooky aboard. Before leaving the sailors had stripped the Baychimo of all food and fuel. If the ice had broken while we were aboard we would have been doomed. It would have been impossible for us to get up steam to use the winches and lower the boats. ... I am pretty sure Jim Allen, at Wainwright, has been aboard while numerous Eskimos probably have swarmed over her as she is swept around the Arctic ocean. Some sailors from the northland went aboard her a few years ago. They said she was completely gutted, and even the ship's safe which once was supposed to have contained several thousand dollars had been forced open."

Melvin's assumptions are likely correct, as a number of people boarded the *Baychimo* in the months immediately following her loss. On August 22, 1932, the *United Press International* reported, "The steamer Baychimo—'Flying Dutchman' of the Arctic Sea—has been sighted, solidly lodged in ice, seven miles west of Point Barrow, word received here said. The Baychimo is a floating treasure-trove of furs. ... Nineteen men today left Point Barrow with sleds and light native boats of skin, hoping to retrieve part of the cargo, it was reported. They faced a hazardous trip over mountainous peaks of ice, stretches of open water, and grinding floes. The Baychimo last was sighted in January. Adventurers at that time risked their lives to take 14 bales of furs from her. They reached Point Barrow with only one bale."

What, one wonders, did the Hudson's Bay Company think of unauthorized men boarding their ship? According to a report published the same day by the *Canadian Press*, not much: "Hudson's Bay Company officials here said today that reappearance of the lost ship Baychimo in the ice off Point Barrow, Alaska, 'Is interesting news but not of direct concern to us.' ... It appeared unlikely the ship would ever be sighted again, insurance underwriters became responsible. 'If any move is made to salvage the Baychimo, it must be by that underwriter,' said Hudson Bay heads."

By March 1933, the *Baychimo* had been swept back to near where she had originally been abandoned. Hoping to salvage some of the furs remaining on board, a team of around 30 Eskimos kayaked out to the ship, only to be trapped on her, without food, for 10 days when a terrible storm blew in. They escaped with their lives but little else.

In the months that followed, stories of various people's adventures on the *Baychimo* turned up from time to time. Then, there was another sighting that summer. Dalton set the stage for the story for readers: "Trader, an impossibly small 10-ton wooden schooner, sailed from Nome, Alaska, each year on trading voyages to settlements on Alaska's west and north coasts, sailing as far as Point Barrow and, when ice conditions permitted, even farther east to Herschel Island in the Yukon. On her July 1933 voyage she carried her owner, Nome merchant Ira Rank, Icelandic skipper Kari Palsson and his brother Pete (the engineer), plus one passenger: Isobel Wylie Hutchison, an adventurous botanist from Scotland, on an expedition to collect Alaskan and Arctic wildflowers. With its limited deck space heavily laden with drums of oil and gasoline, plus containers of fresh fruit and vegetables, Trader was an unlikely vessel to carry a passenger—especially a foreign woman travelling alone—in those days. Moreover, the botanist travelled with her own heavy baggage—a full 300 pounds of it. ... 'I wonder if we shall meet Baychimo this year?' Captain Palsson asked as he and the other three stood on deck watching Northland's progress. Ira Rank said she would probably have drifted to somewhere in Siberian waters by then. Baychimo had last been seen in the ice, well to the west of Point Barrow the previous year, so his assumption had merit, but Ira was wrong. Although she could not be seen,

Baychimo—ghost ship of the Arctic—was closer than any aboard Trader could have imagined."

Suddenly, the ship appeared through the mists like the ghost she was accused of being. Determined to board her, Palsson began to maneuver his ship closer to the mysterious vessel. Isobel Hutchison, a botanist, later recalled, "At last, when success seemed about to desert us, Kari [Captain Palsson] spied a lead turning towards the very cake upon which Baychimo was poised, her giant hull, rust-stained and battered by the frozen seas, looming tower-like above the little Trader. She was riding upon a pan of ice which looked already almost on the verge of breaking up, though it might be that the winter freeze-up would set the stranded ship upon yet another year's wandering."

Isobel Wylie Hutchison

In the wake of that encounter, the *Associated Press* reported, "Isobel Wylie Hutchinson, who collects Arctic specimens for two English institutions, was with one of these two groups, the only white woman ever to have boarded the derelict. The little Scotswoman, perhaps the only white woman who travels the Arctic on her own, was in Halifax today on the way back to England with botanical specimens and Eskimos curios. And she told reporters of her visit aboard the Baychimo when it looked up 12 miles off Wainwright—its starting point—last summer. Miss

Hutchinson was traveling along the coast, in the Beaufort sea, on the little schooner 'Trader' manned by an Icelandic crew. Capt. Peter Palsson steered a perilous course through the floes to the big steamer, lifted almost fully out of the water by the tightly-packed ice. … The hold still contained some caribou skins. The rifled hold, open to the winds, held an odd assortment of…ore, typewriters, curios,…paper, and Hudson's Bay company ledgers. A pair of rusted handcuffs lay on the hatch. In a wooden box rested a 'Times History of the Great War.' 'Trader' was weighed down with salvage when she loft Baychimo's side as night fell. She headed shoreward past the revenue cutter Northland…and soon the Baychimo vanished into the mists. It was several days later that those on the Trader sighted the Baychimo again. Far off on the edge of a glittering ice pack, they saw the phantom ship reflected in a mirage. She was steering at a good five miles an hour past the shoals and ice that held Trader, heading towards Point Barrow with the pack. 'You'd think,' said Capt. Pete, 'that someone was steering her. I guess she's haunted. She steers clear of the shoals as if a master hand was at her wheel.' Trader stayed trapped in the ice 15 days as Baychimo sailed on to her will o' the wisp destination."

The ship was seen again several months later in August 1933 floating along to the north, and on October 22, a news article reported, "LIKE a ghost rising out of the Arctic Ocean, the fur-trading steamship Baychimo—the Flying Dutchman of the Far North—has been sighted again. Men with sleds and light native boats of skin are pushing their way over mountainous peaks of ice stretches of open water and grinding floes with the one desperate hope of retrieving at least a part of the vessel's treasure-trove of furs. But whether success will mark their venture depends entirely upon the constantly changing moods and whims of King Neptune and his traditional lieutenant, Davy Jones. For since last October a year ago…the Baychimo has been the football of the old man of the deep. Unceremoniously, he has booted it hither and yon among the floes of ice. Why he has not seen fit to send her and her million-dollar cargo of luxurious furs plunging down into the Port of Missing Ships deep below the ocean's surface or, if he has, how the sturdy vessel has been able to withstand such efforts is one of the mysteries of the sea, and there are many. Each year deserted ice-locked ships are seen in the polar seas, drifting at the mercy of the wind and current, their broken masts and crumbling rigging hung with icicles and their decks and cabins buried in snow. But they are seldom seen a second time. Davy Jones' locker claims them! But the Baychimo has been the exception to the rule. Three times this sturdy vessel of the Hudson's Bay Company has been sighted…. Once, in February of this year, adventurers risked their lives to take fourteen bales of fur from her hold. When they returned for more, however, the Baychimo had disappeared. Neptune had booted her on her way again! And now once more she has been sighted solidly lodged in the ice, this time west of Point Barrow, and again men are seeking the treasure hoard of fur below her decks."

The next publicized sighting of the *Baychimo* occurred in early July 1934 when a schooner happened up on her and boarded the vessel for a few hours. Their tales only added to her legend, with the *Associated Press* reporting, "The recent sighting of the 'ghost ship' Baychimo near Point Barrow, after she had been lost to the sight of men for a year and a half, calls to mind one of the sea's most captivating mysteries, though a dread menace to every sailor—the derelict, writes Louis H. Bolander in the Baltimore Sun. The Baychimo…was seen again by Eskimos in April, 1932. Since then, so far as the writer knows, no human eye has ever sighted the sturdy steamship, clutched in the remorseless Arctic ice. There is something fascinating, something compelling in the thought of these lonely, broken, shabby sea hoboes drifting over the seven seas at the mercy of wind, tide and current. Though a menace to sober shipping there still clings to them an atmosphere of romance."

By August 1934, *Baychimo* had become the stuff of legends, appearing in the syndicated column "Strange As It Seems," similar to *Ripley's Believe It or Not*. That article noted, "UNCANNILY drifting unharmed through treacherous, ice strewn waters, the derelict trading ship Baychimo has sailed a course determined by chance for three years off Alaska. The ship, property of The Hudson Bay Company, had a valuable cargo of fur aboard when she was lost, but Eskimos and others have boarded her from time to time to salvage what they could—and now, just a few trinkets are to be found. Many a well-manned ship has been caught and crushed by the ice of the arctic in spite of the use of modern navigation aids, but the Baychimo with no one aboard has been undamaged."

Over time, seeing the *Baychimo* became something of a dream for many Arctic sailors, inciting curiosity and anticipation to the point that people actually noticed when the ship did not make her regular appearance. In November 1935, the *Associated Press* reported, seemingly with concern, "Coast guardsmen, home from the far north patrol, said today the entire navigation season passed without a glimpse of the Arctic's 'Flying Dutchman,' the ghost ship Baychimo. It was the second year the fur ship…failed to reappear. But officers and men said the Arctic residents refused to say 'she's gone.' The Baychimo…has reappeared several times between Wainwright and Point Barrow just when given up for lost. … Erased from the register and her insurance paid long before her first reappearance, the Baychimo is officially 'dead.' But she has a habit of resurrection, this derelict of the north."

There were only a few more sightings of the *Baychimo* in the years that followed, until July 1938, when a story came out about the legendary ghost ship: "Unmanned for seven years an ice-sheathed phantom of the Arctic, the world's most famous ghost ship has flashed into view again to revive a story as strange as this crewless vessel itself. For only a few minutes was this wraith-like vessel visible to a few Arctic observers before disappearing again into the mists, to continue cruising in uncharted, ice-locked seas around the North Pole, a voyage that can end only in ultimate destruction. Six times men have seen the ship, since the ice first swept her away from civilization in 1931. How far the vessel has sailed, where it has been, no one can even guess, although the ice apparently carries its prisoner over a similar course each year— a premise borne out by the fact that the ghost has been sighted three times off Point Barrow, at varying distances ranging from seven to 10 miles away. Never before in the history of the North, seafaring men say, has a vessel survived more than two seasons in the crushing, grinding, shifting chaos of the

Polar ice. Each time the ghost is seen the appearance is proclaimed as definitely live last. But the ghost sails on. What is the story of this fantastic craft, that has successfully defied the elements for seven years? This astonishingly vital ghost ship is the 1300-ton iron steamer Baychimo, owned by the Hudson Bay Company, and for nine years the only link between the 'outside' and the remote fur trading posts inside the Arctic Circle."

Anthony Dalton described the last confirmed sighting of the *Baychimo*, a full three decades after the ship had been abandoned: "In the summer of 1962 a party of Inupiat in kayaks glided silently along a lead on the Beaufort Sea, just offshore from the north Alaskan coast…As the horizon changed from a miniature mountain range of rafted ice to a more level field, they could see a large black shape beyond, becoming more visible with each moment. A ship stuck in the ice. Her name, rusting but readable, was a dirty scar on her bow: Baychimo."

There were no other likely sightings of the *Baychimo*, and over the years people finally began to accept that she likely went down somewhere in the Arctic after that sighting in the early 1960s. However, the fact that she is now almost certainly under the sea instead of on it has in no way discouraged adventurers from looking for her. As late as May 2006, a newspaper story reported hope of finding the Baychimo by means of an Alaskan government project for historic shipwrecks.

Nonetheless, in spite of those and many other efforts, the *Baychimo* seems to have given mankind all the information she is going to at this time. After roaming the seas for years in a nautical purgatory, she seems to have finally found her resting place at the bottom of the ocean. Only time will tell if there will be fresh new sightings of the Arctic's most famous ghost ship.

Online Resources

Other mystery titles by Charles River Editors

Other titles about the *Mary Celeste* on Amazon

Other books about the Baychimo on Amazon

Bibliography

Begg, Paul (2007). *Mary Celeste: The Greatest Mystery of the Sea*. Harlow, Essex: Pearson Education Ltd.

Conan Doyle, Arthur, *J. Habakuk Jephson's Statement*

Dalton, Anthony, *Baychimo: Arctic Ghost Ship*, Heritage House, 2006.

Fay, Charles Edey (1988). *The Story of the Mary Celeste*. New York: Dover Publications.

Gunston, David (August 1991). "The ghost ship of the Arctic" (PDF). The UNESCO Courier: a window open on the world. XLIV: 63–65.

Harper, Kenn (November 24, 2006). "Ghost Ship: The Disappearance of the Baychimo". Nunatsiaq News.

Hastings, Macdonald (1972). *Mary Celeste*. London: Michael Joseph.

Hicks, Brian (2004). *Ghost Ship: The Mysterious True Story of the Mary Celeste and her Missing Crew*. New York: Random House.

Free Books by Charles River Editors

We have brand new titles available for free most days of the week. To see which of our titles are currently free, click on this link.

Discounted Books by Charles River Editors

We have titles at a discount price of just 99 cents everyday. To see which of our titles are currently 99 cents, click on this link.

Printed in Great Britain
by Amazon